Great Cycle Routes

Cumbria and North Yorkshire

Jeremy Evans

The Crowood Press

First published in 1996 by
The Crowood Press Ltd
Ramsbury, Marlborough
Wiltshire SN8 2HR

British Library Cataloguing-in-Publication Data
A catalogue record for this book is available from the British Library.

ISBN 1 85223 947 6

Picture Credits
All photographs by Jeremy Evans
Map-drawings by Dave Ayres

Printed and bound by J. W. Arrowsmith Ltd, Bristol

Contents

Introduction

RIDE INFORMATION

Area: Where the ride is located.

OS Map: The relevant OS Landranger 1:50,000 map for the route.

Route: Waymarks from start to finish, with OS grid reference numbers. All of the rides in this book are circular, making it possible to start at a number of locations.

Nearest BR Stations: Most of the routes are accessible from a railway station. Check restrictions and costs before you start.

Approx Length: In miles and kilometres. There should always be some allowance for getting lost or altering the route.

Time: This is very difficult to assess, and will depend on factors such as whether the tracks are dry, how many hills have to be climbed, how fast you ride, and how many pubs and places of interest there are en route.

Rating: An 'Easy' ride should be accessible for riders of all abilities, excluding sub-teenage children; a 'Moderate' ride may prove harder in terms of terrain, length, hills, churning those pedals, and possibly navigation; a 'Hard' ride is best suited to experienced offroad riders with a high level of commitment. However these ratings can be changed by the weather - for instance an 'Easy' ride in very dry weather may become a 'Hard' ride when the tracks are churned to mud.

Places to Visit/Pubs and Cafés: Virtually all of these rides feature a number of possible pub and café stops and other attractions.

If you wish to hire a bike, a directory of cycle hire outlets is available free from the Cyclists' Touring Club. Send a large SAE to: CTC, 69 Meadrow, Godalming, Surrey, GU7 3HS.

COMMON SENSE OFFROAD

The tracks and trails used for offroad cycling must be shared. The basic problems for mountain bikers is that bikes are generally so much faster than walkers and horse-riders. That is the principal factor which causes antagonism, but why hurry? Why not take it easy and enjoy the ride? Stick to the following common sense rules, and everyone should be happy.

1. Stay on public bridleways, byways or roads. Never ride on footpaths. Cycling on private tracks or open ground is not usually allowed without permission from the landowner. Always moderate your speed.

2. When you ride offroad, the bridleways and byways are classified as 'Highways'. This means the Highway Code applies, and you can be prosecuted for riding dangerously, especially if you are involved in an accident. Any form of racing is illegal on a public highway, unless it is a specially organized event and permission has been obtained. Byways may also be shared with motorized vehicles. They should give way to cyclists, but as when meeting any vehicle, it is necessary to play safe.

3. Learn how to prevent skids and ride with control to help prevent erosion, especially in the wet. If it is very wet, it is much better to push or carry your bike. Going off the official tracks and trails can cause unnecessary erosion, as well as damaging plant and animal environments.

4. When you meet other people offroad and in the countryside, be courteous and considerate. Always slow right down and give way to both walkers and horse-riders, even if it means dismounting and lifting your bike out of the way. Bikes are almost silent, so give warning of your approach in as polite a manner as possible. The British Horse Society would like you to 'Hail a Horse'; we think the very best policy is to come to a complete halt until the animals have passed you by. If you are riding in a group, all go

one side of the track. Take particular care when you ride past children – you may not worry them, but you may terrorize/infuriate their parents.

5. Make sure your bike is safe to ride, and won't let you down in the middle of nowhere on a fast downhill – learn basic maintenance and take essential spares. In the interests of safety take drink and food, and wear suitable clothing for the weather conditions and length of ride. It is wise to wear a helmet, putting a layer of polystyrene between your cranium and any hard object in the unlikely event of a bad fall.

6. To avoid getting lost, it is always wise to carry a compass and relevant map such as the OS 1:50,000 Landranger series. You should know where you are, and have the ability to re-plan the route and cut the ride short.

7. Follow the Country Code. Leave nothing behind - no litter, noorange peel, the minimum of noise, no bad memories for yourself or for others, and if possible not even a sign of your wheeltracks. Always shut gates behind you (unless they should obviously be left open). Don't blast through fields of cows or sheep - neither they nor the farmer will like it. If you ride with a dog for a companion, keep it under control.

USE THAT MAP!

Unless the route is very easy or you know it well, you should never ride without a map, never ride without a compass. Once you get the hang of it, using them is easy and will ensure you know where you're heading.

A map is a diagram which shows the fea-

safe! Don't ride into danger.

tures of an area of land such as mountains, hills, woods, rivers, railways, roads, tracks, towns and buildings. All these and many other features are shown by special signs that map readers can understand. There is always a table on the map which explains the signs. On a 1:50, 000 map (OS Landranger) 1cm on the map equals 50,000cm on the ground; this equals 2cm for every kilometre, or 1¹/₄in per mile.

THE GRID SYSTEM: Maps are covered by a grid of numbered horizontal and vertical grid lines. The grid is used to find an exact place on a map. To find a grid reference position you read the first three numbers off the vertical grid line which is called the Eastings line. You then read the next three numbers off the horizontal Northings grid line. Where they meet is where you want to be.

CONTOURS: Contours are lines on a map which join areas that are the same height above sea level (in metres). The difference in height between the contour lines is called the vertical height. The closer the lines are the steeper the hill will be. Contour lines are spaced at 10m intervals on 1:50, 000 Landranger maps, and at 5m intervals on 1:25, 000 Outdoor Leisure maps.

It is generally best to arrange your ride so the climbs are short and steep and the descents are long and fast; it is also best to get major climbs out of the way early on the ride. Sometimes it is quite difficult to know if you will be going up or down; a river or stream on the map is a sure sign of dropping down to a valley, but you can also work it out by looking at the contour line height numbers, as the top of the number is always uphill.

USING A COMPASS: A compass is a valuable aid to finding your way. The most popular style is the Swedish-made Silva on which most modern hiking (equally suitable for biking) compasses are based. It is low in price, light, very tough, and easy to use.

The compass should be carried on a lanyard at all times; in bad visibility it may be the only means you have of finding the way. The compass needle always points to Magnetic North, but keep it away from close contact with any metallic object to which it might be sensitive. Knowing that the needle points North, you can always follow a course in the direction you wish to go. The vertical grid lines on a map point to Grid North; this may be a few degrees different from Magnetic North, but the difference is very small.

OFFROAD WITH KIDS

Why not take the kids with you? With a little care the whole family can have a great day out, and when the kids are too big for a child seat you can put them in the saddle and still stay in control.

There's no point in taking children cycling on-road or offroad if they don't enjoy it, because then you won't enjoy it. Always follow the three golden rules:

1. Make sure they're comfortable.

2. Keep them amused.

3. Don't bite off more than you can chew.

COMFORT: For a child up to around four years of age, go for the best rear-mounted child seat you can find. It must obviously be secure on the bike, with a high back and sides to help protect its occupant if you should fall, deep footwells to protect the feet, and a full harness to hold the child firmly in; a safety bar for the child to grip on to is also a worthwhile extra. Ideally, the seat should also be quick and easy to put on and take off your bike, so when you ride alone the seat doesn't have to go with you.

It's a good idea to get children used to wearing helmets as early as possible, but with very young children (under one year old) there is a often a problem making the helmet stay on. This results in a miserable baby with a helmet tipped down over its eyes; best then to do without the helmet and be extra careful, until you can be sure it will sit comfortably in position.

Make sure the straps of a helmet are sufficiently tight. Children won't like you fiddling under their chins, and your best policy is to train them to put on and take off the helmet themselves as young as possible, ensuring the straps are adjusted to the right length. Shop around for a child helmet and do ask to try it on. As with most adult helmets, removable rubber pads are used to alter the internal diameter, but the most important consideration is that the design of the helmet and its straps hold it firmly on the head. Some helmets seem to want to slide forward on impact, which is useless.

The child is protected from the headwind by your body, but can still get pretty cold sitting there doing nothing; in winter, an all-in-one waterproof/windproof coverall suit does the job really well. Remember that young children require all sorts of extras – extra clothes, nappies, drink, apples, and so on. Try to keep their requirements down to an acceptable minimum; a neat solution is to carry extras in a small backpack that mounts behind the child seat itself.

KEEP THEM HAPPY: Young children generally love riding on the back of bikes, and want to tell you all about what's going on. It can be bad enough understanding them at the best of times, but in this situation it becomes ridiculous and your replies degenerate to a meaningless 'Yes' or 'No'.

With that level of conversation a child will only sit happily in its seat for so long, especially if it's freezing and foul. Children like regular stops if they're to stay happy, so take a stash of little treats – apples, nuts and raisins, and so on – and ensure that you get to the picnic or pub (make sure they allow children) on time with the shortest part of the ride left for the end of the day.

Routes should be chosen with care and an

A child seat can be a lot of fun.

eye on safety. A rock-strewn 'downhill extreme', which is just waiting to throw you over the handlebars, should obviously be avoided. To start with, keep to mellow and easy offroad routes such as those found in the New Forest or an old railway line such as the Downs Link in Sussex. Moderate uphills are all right when the weight of the child helps back wheel traction; immoderate uphills are plain stupid, as you wheeze and groan pushing both bike and child together.

What about downhills? As long as you're in control there's no danger in going fast on a smooth track or road. Rather than hitting the brakes, it's better to treat it as a laugh and teach the child to get used to the thrill of safe speed.

There comes a time when children grow too big and bored for a conventional rear-mounted seat, but too young to ride their own bike and keep pace (and keep safe) with adults. One answer is the Trailerbike, a remarkable hybrid, which claims it will take children from four to ten years old with a maximum weight of 42kg (6.5 stone). It allows you to ride with your child; they get all the fun of riding their own bike, but you have total control over their speed, where they go, and ultimately their safety. They can also pedal as much or as little as they like. If they have the muscle and aptitude, they'll help push you uphill as well as down.

OFFROAD RIGHTS OF WAY IN ENGLAND & WALES

PUBLIC BRIDLEWAYS: Open to walkers and horse-riders, and also to cyclists since 1968. This right is not sacrosanct; bike bans are possible if riders are considered too much of a nuisance.

PUBLIC BYWAYS: Usually unsurfaced tracks open to cyclists, walkers, horse-riders and vehicles which have right of access to houses.

PUBLIC FOOTPATHS: No rights to cycle. You probably have the right to push a bike, but the temptation to ride is high and in general it is best to avoid footpaths whenever possible.

FORESTRY COMMISSION: Access on designated cycle paths, or by permission from the local Forest Manager. At present there is a general presumption in favour of bikes using Forestry land gratis; this may change.

DESIGNATED CYCLE PATHS: Specially built cycle tracks for urban areas; or using Forestry Commission land or disused railway lines. Cycling is illegal on pavements. However it is frequently much safer and more pleasant, and with the proviso that you take great care to avoid pedestrians (who are seldom seen on out-of-town pavements), we suggest that using pavements can be perfectly reasonable.

WHAT IF BRIDLEWAYS & BYWAYS ARE BLOCKED?

Cyclists are used to being on the defensive on Britain's roads; offroad they should stand up for their rights. The relevant landowner and local authority have the responsibility to maintain bridleways and byways and ensure they are passable with gates that work. It is illegal for a landowner to block a right of way, close or divert it (only the local authority or central government can do this), or put up a misleading notice to deter you from using it.

Abide by the rules – never ride on footpaths.

It is also illegal to plough up or disturb the surface of a right of way unless it is a footpath or bridleway running across a field. In that case the farmer must make good the surface within twenty-four hours or two weeks if it is the first disturbance for a particular crop. A bridleway so restored must have a minimum width of two metres, and its line must be clearly apparent on the ground. A farmer also has a duty to prevent any crops other than grass making a right of way difficult to follow. A bridleway across crops should have a two metre clear width; a field edge bridleway should have a clear width of three metres.

If you run into difficulty on any of the above, you can file a complaint with the Footpaths Officer at the local council, giving full details of the offence and a precise map reference.

OFFROAD CARE AND REPAIR

Have you decided on your route, got the right OS map, and your compass? Have you got all the right clothes, ready for rain, wind or sun, plus food and sufficient drink if it's going to be hot? That just leaves your bike so don't risk getting let down by a breakdown...

BRAKE CHECK: The most important part of your bike - if the brakes fail, you could be dead. Check the blocks for wear, turn them or change them as necessary. Lubricate the cables, check they won't slip, and if there is any sign of fraying, change them. Lube the brake pivots – if the spring return on the brakes isn't working well, they will need to be stripped down and cleaned.

WHEELS: Check your tyres for general wear and side-wall damage; look for thorns. If a wheel is out of line or dented, it needs to be adjusted with a spoke key; also check for loose spokes. Always carry a pump and a puncture repair kit.

CHAIN CARE: Give your chain a regular lube – there are all sorts of fancy spray lubes around, some of which cost a lot of money; however, although the more universal sorts are cheap and reliable, they do attract the dirt. If your chain and cogs are manky, clean them with a rag soaked in spray lubricant or a special 'chain bath'; adjust stiff links with a chain breaker.

MOVING PARTS: Clean and lube the derailleur jockey wheels and gear cogs. Lube the freewheel with the bike on its side. Clean and lube the chainwheel gear mechanism. Lube and check the cables for both sets of gears. Lube the bottom bracket – the most basic method is to pour heavy oil down the top tube. Lube the pedals by taking off the end caps. Check that both the cranks and headset are tight. Check that the derailleur lines up properly.

Other things that may go wrong include

Left: Always prepare your bike carefully.

breaking the chain or having a cable slip, though if you take care of your bike these occurrences are very rare. Just in case, however, it is wise to carry a chainlink extractor which rejoins a broken chain, 4/5/6mm Allen keys, a small adjustable spanner, and a screwdriver with both a flat head and a Phillips head. The neat solution is a 'multi-tool' includes all these items in one package.

PUNCTURE REPAIR

The most common offroad repair is a puncture and the most common cause is the hawthorn. To cope with this you need a pump, tyre levers and a puncture repair kit; you may also like to carry a spare tube. Always go for a full size pump with the correct valve fitting; the pump should fit inside the frame, ideally on the down tube. A double action pump puts in the air the fastest. Two tyre levers are sufficient, either in plastic or metal, whilst a spare tube saves the hassle of finding the leak and doing a patch offroad – unless you are unlucky enough to puncture twice.

1. Stop as soon as you feel a tyre go soggy: riding on a flat tyre is asking for trouble. Find a suitable place to do the repair – well away from any cars – and turn the bike upside-down. Take

Mending the tube is usually a quick operation.

care you know where you put things down: it is too easy to lose that little black screw cap that covers the valve.

2. Undo the brake cable near the brake block, flip off the quick release lever at the hub, and remove the wheel. This is more of a fiddle with the back wheel, and it may be necessary to partly unscrew the hub.

3. You won't get the tube out unless it is well deflated. Carefully insert a lever to get the tyre wall off the rim, and then work the rim off all the way round one side using two levers.

4. Pull the tube out of the tyre. The next thing is to find the puncture. Inflate the tube, and then slowly pass it close to your ear and cheek. you should hear or feel the leak and be able to locate it. If this fails, you can try submerging the tube in a puddle and watch for tell-tale bubbles.

5. When you've found the puncture, keep a finger on it so you don't lose it. Roughen the surrounding area with the 'roughener' provided in your repair kit, and then cover the area with a patch sized blob of glue. Now leave the glue to set.

6. To find out what caused the puncture, run your fingers round the inside of the tyre; the probable cause is a thorn which is still in the tyre. Remove it carefully.

7. The glue should now be set enough to put on the patch which should bond straight to the tube. If it seems OK, partly inflate the tube, which makes things easier when getting the tyre back onto the rim.

8. Reassemble the wheel and put it back on the bike. Connecting the brake cable first ensures the wheel is centred by a pull on the brake lever before you tighten the quick release hub; it also ensures you don't ride off with the brake undone. Now inflate the tyre fully.

SAFETY OFFROAD

The first rule of offroad touring is to allow enough time. Getting caught by nightfall is foolhardy and potentially dangerous, particularly if the ride ends in an on-road section and you have no lights. So before you leave, work out how much time to allow, and be pessimistic. Your speed will depend on your skill, level of fitness, and the riding conditions.

Tackling a route after heavy rain in midwinter may take three times as long as the same route in dry summer weather. Riding along a disused railway line will be fast and easy; riding up and down big hills can be exceptionally demanding, and the difference in speed between a good and not so good rider will be much greater.

Riding in a group should ensure some degree of safety, but groups which are much bigger than three riders bring their own problems. They can put an unacceptable load on other people's enjoyment of the environment; walkers and horseriders were there first, and while they can cope with small groups of bike riders, it's no fun for them when a dozen or so Tour de France lookalikes blast through their favourite countryside. By contrast riding alone has much to recommend it; you cause minimum upset to others, and also don't have to worry about keeping up with the fastest member of the group, while the slowest rider doesn't have to worry about keeping up with you.

Whether you ride alone or in a small group, before leaving the golden rule is *tell someone:*
- When you're going.
- When you expect to be back.
- Give them some idea of your route.

It doesn't happen often, but riders do occasionally fall off and knock themselves out or break a few bones in the middle of nowhere; if that happened to you, it would be nice to know that someone would come looking for you, and that they'd be able to locate you before too long.

A First Aid kit is only of value if someone knows how to use it, and even then the constrictions of space and weight on a bike will make its

Don't race unless it's official.

application limited; some bandages and plasters will be enough to deal with minor cuts and abrasions, or possibly support a fracture. In most cases injuries from falls are fairly minor, and you can keep on riding; in more serious cases it will probably be a case of getting help ASAP, while caring for the injured rider:

• If two crash, help the worst injured first.

• If a rider is unconscious, don't leave him on his back. Use the First Aid 'recovery position' if you know how, and cover him with a coat if possible. If a rider is unconscious and not breathing, give the kiss of life if you know how.

• Staunch any bleeding by applying a pad or hand pressure; if bleeding is in an arm or leg, raise the injured limb unless broken.

• Don't move the rider if he seems to be paralysed, unless in immediate danger.

• Don't give the rider anything to eat, drink or smoke.

• Don't leave the injured rider alone.

If you ride regularly it's well worth attending a full length course to get a First Aid certificate which is valid for three years. These are run all round the UK by organizations such as the British Red Cross Society, whose phone number can be found in the local telephone directory.

Cumbria

Cumbria is the land of the English Lake District, renowned the world over for its high hills, deep valleys and wonderful stretches of water. You have to go up to get the views, but while some of the eight Lakeland rides included here are tough and demand hard riding there are others that can be enjoyed by less committed riders who can work up from the easy forestry circuits of Grizedale Forest.

Ride 9 is different in that it leaves the Lakes to cross the M6 and venture into the quiet but very wild country to the east, via a section of the Cumbria Cycleway; this leaves the road and crosses the Pennines by a magnificent route. Further challenging rides are suggested to help the more intrepid biker explore this interesting area, which gets away from the honeypot crowds of the Lakes.

Ride 1: Round Buttermere

Ride 2: Offroad and Uphill to Helvellyn

Ride 3: East of Ullswater

Ride 4: Up and down Loadpot Hill

Ride 5: High Street: Ullswater to Windermere

Ride 6: A Tour of Grizedale Forest

Ride 7: Round Ennerdale

Ride 8: Round Coniston

Ride 9: Over the Pennines

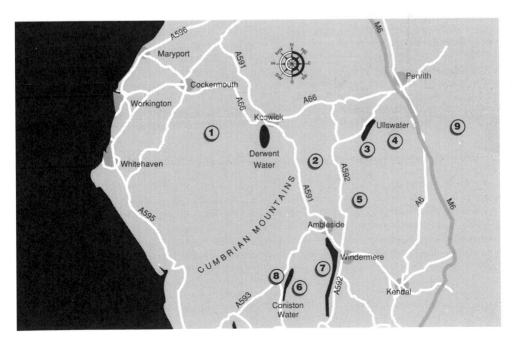

1 Round Buttermere

Offroad and On-Road

Area: The Lake District. A ride round Buttermere and beyond. Start and finish at Buttermere at GR:175170; alternatively start from Gatesgarth Farm CP at GR:196150.

OS Map: Outdoor Leisure 4 – The English Lakes North Western area; Landranger 89 – West Cumbria.

Route:
Buttermere (GR:175170)
Newlands Hause (GR:195177)
Rigg Beck (GR:228201)
Little Town (GR:233195)
Hause Gate (GR:245192)
Grange (GR:252175)
Castle Crag (GR:248158)
Little Gatesgarthdale (GR:237138)
Honister Hause (GR:226135)
Gatesgarth Farm (GR:196150)
Scale Bridge (GR:168166)
Buttermere (GR:175170)

Nearest BR Station:
None within easy reach.

Nearest Youth Hostel:
Buttermere or Honister Hause.

Approx Length: 30 miles (48km).

Time: Allow 4 hours plus stops.

Rating: Hard. There are some technical offroad sections, but this is great country, with fine views. There are three big climbs.

This ride divides into three offroad sections, with two long on-road sections sandwiched between them. The on-road riding is very pleasant, passing through some of the Lake District's most spectacular countryside with mind boggling descents – you've never been so fast – and comparatively few cars to worry about. The offroad riding is tough by comparison!

1. The ride starts from Buttermere, and takes the minor road to the north-east on a long uphill to Newlands Hause, a steady climb with dramatic scenery all the way. From the top the route runs fast downhill in the lee of Knott Rigg, then flattens out following several twists and turns, coming eventually to the turning to Little Town over on the right in the valley.

2. This turn down a narrow lane is almost impossible to miss: a most unusual lilac-painted clapperboard house is on the corner, which looks like it has flown straight in from the southern states of the USA! Turn right down to Little Town; there is a pleasant diversion for those who feel so inclined, along the right turn signposted to the small church, a most attractive building set in charming surroundings. Then carry on along the road to Little Town, past a stile on the right and climbing uphill past a few houses. The bridleway goes up through a gate just beyond these; it is marked 'Footpath', but is clearly used as a bridleway.

3. The track bears right and left uphill, keeping to the right side of the hillside on a good surface; it then crosses the stream below Yewthwaite Crag and continues up the other side. For some way here it is unridable, but it improves nearer the top; Derwent Water comes into sight ahead as the route crosses a footpath; this path leads left up to the hill called Cat Bells, and right steeply up to High Ground.

4. Go straight on here, joining the track that leads down the hillside from Hause Gate. This is easy to follow, as much of it is marked by rail-

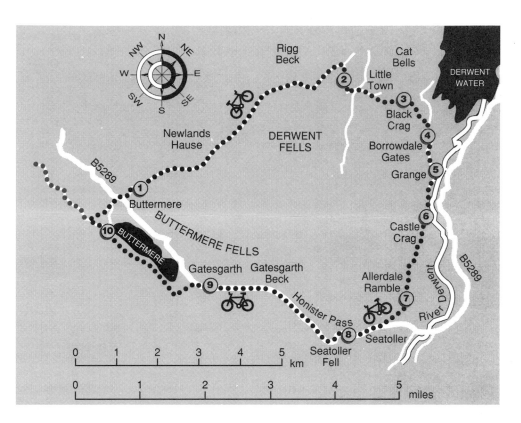

ings, but the first part is ferociously steep – one would imagine too difficult for horses – and all the way down it is tricky until the lower sections; here it joins the road running along the west side of Buttermere.

5. Turn right here, and the route soon runs back into Grange, an attractive little village popular with summer trippers and served by a cafe, a tea-house, a shop, a chapel and a hotel. Just before you reach the bends that lead to the bridge over the River Derwent, look out for a bridleway sign pointing down a track to the right. Take this, following it straight ahead and ignoring a fork going off to the right. Head up through woods and then down to the side of the River Derwent close by a campsite; from here, follow the bridleway on as indicated by a blue arrow pointing uphill.

6. As the track climbs, it steadily gets worse, becoming increasingly rocky as it heads up Broadslack Gill towards Castle Crag. This old road can only be ridden with extreme difficulty, but persevere nevertheless, pushing if necessary. At the top, the views all around are quite magnificent, with Derwent Water behind and Borrowdale spread out before you.

7. At the top you join a grass track, and from here on it is mainly downhill and most of the route is ridable, although rocky sections do sometimes make the going difficult. Where the main track appears to bear right, around the hillside, take the narrower track which runs downhill to cross the bridge over Tongue Gill; go carefully here, because this is part of the 'Allerdale Ramble' and at weekends there may be several walkers. Beyond the footbridge the

Buttermere is one of the most magnificent sights of the Lake District, and best viewed from a bike.

track starts to head downhill, and becomes easier, eventually coming into sight of the road at Seatoller; here, go through a gate: the footpath goes straight down to the road, while the bridleway bears round to the right, following alongside the road and joining it some way on.

8. Once on-road at Little Gatesgarthdale, the worst part of the climb is behind you; however, there is still some way to go to the youth hostel at the top of Honister Hause. From here the on-road descent along Honister Pass is a quite unforgettable experience: it drops down very steeply, then levels out on a seemingly endless downhill run nearly all the way to Gatesgarth Farm and Cottage at the south-eastern end of Buttermere. (This is an alternative start for the ride; there is ample parking.) The final offroad section starts here.

9. Turn left through a gate, following the track ahead which runs across the bottom of Buttermere with the mighty presence of High Crag towering ahead of you. Past another gate the bridleway forks: left is a very stiff uphill climb to Scarth Gap Pass; right follows the shore of Buttermere. Take this latter route, which is relatively easy riding, although occasional rocky sections make progress more difficult, and on a summer weekend your progress will almost certainly be slowed by walkers. Some way along the bridleway bears left to go

slightly uphill through Burtness Wood, while a 'Permissive Path' continues by the lakeside. Follow the bridleway, and then take the first turning right; from here the route runs downhill and brings you back down to the lake.

10. A short way on you come to the waterfalls at Sourmilk Gill, where a bridleway is signposted going left steeply uphill to Red Pike. Follow the bridleway straight ahead: a fairly rocky section leads to the shores of Crummock Water in splendid isolated scenery. From here a bridleway goes up, up and over to Ennerdale Water on the other side of the hills, but unless you enjoy it very tough it is not at all suitable for bike riding. Instead go back a short distance to Scale Bridge; from here a bridleway to Buttermere is a good, flat track. At Buttermere there is a hotel, a tea shop and a youth hostel – and plenty of trippers on a summer afternoon!

Places to Visit:
Nearest Information Centre at Keswick which also boasts a museum, the Beatrix Potter's Lake District exhibition (NT – tel: 017687 75173) and the Castlerigg Stone Circle (NT) on its outskirts.

Pubs and Cafés:
Pub and cafés at Grange and Buttermere.

---

2 Offroad and Uphill to Helvellyn

**Offroad and
On-Road**

Area: The Lake District. A tour of the fells to the north-east of Helvellyn. Start and Finish at Glenridding at the southern end of Ullswater. There is plenty of car parking if you get there early.

OS Map: Outdoor Leisure 5 – The English Lakes North Eastern area; Landranger 90 – Penrith, Keswick & Ambleside area.

Route:
Glenridding (GR:387168)
A592/A5091 turn-off (GR:399198)
Aira Falls CP (GR:410201)
Dockray turn-off (GR:393216)
Groovebeck Fold (GR:372221)
Matterdale Common (GR.350213)
Great Dodd (GR:343204)
Watson's Dodd (GR:340195)
Raise (GR:343174)
Whiteside Bank (GR:337167)
Helvellyn (GR:342152)
Glenridding Common (GR:357170)
Greenside Road (GR:370174)
Glenridding (GR:387168)

Nearest BR Station: Penrith.

Nearest Youth Hostel:
Patterdale.

Approx Length: 15 miles (24km).

Time: Allow 3 hours.

Rating: Hard. This is one serious climb on the way up and some of the route is technically tricky on the way down, but you can't get much higher.

This is a fine circuit, heading up towards the mighty Helvellyn with views that get more fantastic by the mile. It is predictably hard, climbing upwards to its highest point of 3,000ft (880m). It is ridable all the way bar about fifty yards up the final rocky slope at Raise, but to keep on riding you need to be good, fit and motivated; however, pushing is no hardship since the landscape is so fine. With this in mind, only attempt this circuit on a clear day. The ground is very exposed and the usual precautions should be taken. The first half of the ride down is also very rocky, so take it easy.

1.   Start from Glenridding at the southern end of Ullswater. From here, ride just over 2 miles (3.2km) along the A592 lakeside road to the A5091 turn-off. Alternatively if Glenridding is full, you can start from the Aira Force waterfalls car park towards the western end of the north shore of Ullswater on the A592 lakeside road, a short distance east of the A5091 turning to Dockray.

2.   Turn onto the A5091; it is now a long climb uphill from base camp at 510ft (150m). Follow the road up into open country, and after just over a mile you come to Dockray. Turn left by the inn on the corner – stop if you like, but there's still a long way to go – and take the narrower lane towards Gill Edge. Follow it for about ³/₄ mile (1.2km); then where it bends right around the edge of the woods at Red Moss, carry straight on ahead through a gate, joining a track which runs along the left-hand side of the woods.

3.   Beyond the woods the track heads out into open country with a hill ahead, and then turns right across a footbridge over Groove Beck at Groovebeck Fold. A few yards further on a much rougher track bears left off the main track; follow it uphill, and keep following it as it swings west-south-west across Matterdale Common. The going is not too steep, but the surface

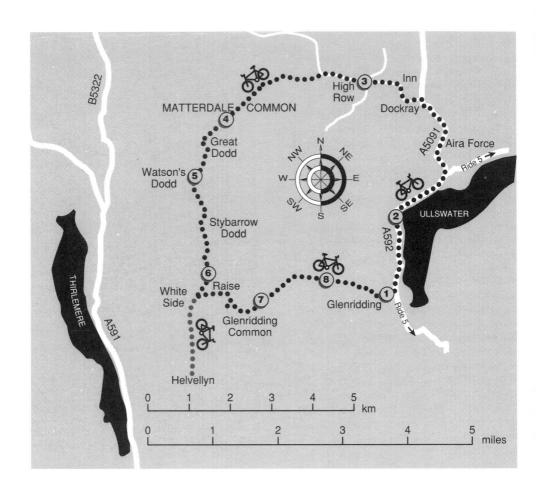

is variable, boggy with soft grass in places to slow you down. However, it is easy to follow, cutting a narrow path across the moor with big hills up ahead.

4. Keep on, and this path comes to a small plateau by the side of Randerside, a rock-strewn outcrop to the left. Ahead is Great Dodd, and the track to follow climbs straight up its steep side over to the right - a fairly awesome sight. The summit is marked by a conspicuous cairn, while over to the left is a shelter cairn offering protection from the prevailing south-westerly winds.

5. From the top of Great Dodd you can see the track snaking up and down the hillsides ahead in a southerly direction. First it heads down Millgill Head, before bearing right to Watson's Dodd where it starts to head up again along the side of Stybarrow Dodd with intermittent cairns showing the way. It then drops steeply downhill to Sticks Pass, before the last great climb up a particularly severe hill called Raise. Those who wish to ride up should bear over to the right where the going is easiest; only the last 50 yards (45m) or so become unrideable because of loose rocks and a very steep angle.

The ride to the top is steady but hard, which makes a long downhill something to look forward to.

This track heads down the hillside to the mountain rescue centre. Take care on loose rock!

6. On the far side of Raise the full magnificence of Helvellyn comes into view, bearing round to the left ahead of you and frequently looking like a dark, brooding mass. To the right is Thirlmere and to the left Ullswater; if the weather is good the view on all sides is magnificent. Head downhill on the track ahead, coming to a cairn at the bottom where the track starts to go up Whiteside Bank. The top of Helvellyn is about a mile distant, but the going gets harder and it makes better sense to leave your bike and walk it to the 950m trig point if you want to see what the summit is like. Beyond it a bridleway goes down to Glenridding via Dollywagon Pike, but it is very steep and rocky and is not recommended for biking.

7. Looking east from the cairn at Whiteside there is a clear track running down along the left side of the valley above Red Screes and Keppel Cove. This will take you down to Glenridding in fairly quick time, but the track which zig-zags its way down the hillside is covered in loose rock and requires careful riding – if in doubt, walk it! At the bottom of the zig-zags it straightens out and improves as it drops lower in the valley; it crosses a footbridge and then bears right, continuing to descend in a short series of more graceful zig-zags to the mountain rescue/outdoor pursuits centre below old mine workings.

8. From the mountain rescue centre the track heads straight down Greenside Road on a good surface, passing over a cattle grid with cottages on the left as it joins a tarmac road. Keep left downhill, and you soon come into Glenridding where there are plenty of tea shops and cafés to replenish your strength.

> **Places to Visit:**
> As a diversion, try the Ullswater lake steamers which call at Glenridding; the Aira Force waterfalls (NT car park off the A592) are also worth a visit.
>
> **Pubs and Cafés:**
> Pubs and cafés at Glenridding; pub at Dockray.

left and on up.

5. This a long hill. I preferred to push, and in some parts it is steep even then! At the top is the flat, level area called Boredale Hause with the ruins of a few old mine workings; it is a good place to stop and rest. From here on a compass is handy to make sure you are heading in the right direction. Head due east from Boredale Hause, and then take the right-hand one of two tracks going south-east. This leads you round the side of Red Scar heading along the edge of Beda Fell, and should not be confused with the track that heads north-east down the side of Hawk Crag. This leads to Boredale Head, and is the way to go if you want to cut the distance for a more direct return.

6. Keep on heading steadily upwards to the top of Bedafell Knott; it is a long way but the views from the summit are stunning. A track appears to go on along the ridge, but you want the one that goes down the other side into the Bannerdale Valley, opening out a magnificent view to the south and leading down to the farmstead at Dale Head. The track passes a lonely ruin, and then heads on downhill on a mainly grass surface – most of it is easily ridable but parts can be tricky and it is not the sort of descent for great speeds.

7. At Dale Head go through the old farmyard, joining the lane which runs along the valley to the farmstead at Winter Crag, and on past the old chapel with fabulous views behind until you come out on the road close to Hallin Fell which you rode past on the outward route. Turn right here, and then right again by the small church, joining a bridleway which goes directly up a steep short hill. At the top, push on in the same direction; this leads you up and over a hillock to a fast track that runs down towards Howtown.

8. When you come to a cattle grid by bridleway signs, you have the choice of going down to Howtown – where there is a pub with a walkers' bar which should be suitable for your battered

and muddy state – or carrying straight on as directed over the stream. If you go to Howtown don't bottle out and ride on-road back to Pooley Bridge. The offroad section which follows is probably the most enjoyable of the ride, so backtrack to follow the offroad route.

9. Go through a gate by a smart house at Mellguards, joining the track which runs by the side of a wall more or less parallel to the lake. Mostly it's quite fast going until you come to a right and left fork – the left says Pooley Bridge and is downhill; the right says Moor Divock and is very much uphill. Despite this, the Moor Divock route is the way to go as the Pooley Bridge fork takes you down to the road some 3 miles (5km) from the village.

10. Ride on up by the side of Auterstone Crag beneath the might of Arthur's Fell, a spectacular rock overhang, and continue to follow the clear track through ferns and across the moor. It soon levels out, and offers fast riding past Barton Park Wood and on to 'The Cockpit' circle of stones. From here you turn left to join the main track by a four-way bridleway sign (straight on if you want to ride back via bridleway towards Penrith), turning left for a fast and furious final descent towards Pooley Bridge. After that it's straight on down the lane for half a mile or so before you are back in Pooley Bridge.

Places to Visit:
As a diversion, try the Ullswater lake steamers which call at Howtown Wyke en route from Pooley ridge to Glenridding.

Pubs and Cafés:
Pub and cafés at Pooley Bridge;
serious food in opulent surroundings at Sharrow Bay (bikers should change for a meal here);
pubs at Patterdale and Howtown;
small seasonal cafe at Side Farm.

4 Up and Down Loadpot Hill

Mainly Offroad

Area: The north-east Lake District. A second tour of the fells to the east and Ullswater. Start and finish at Pooley Bridge at the northern end of Ullswater. Limited car parking. For rail access start and finish at Penrith using connecting route from Ride 5.

OS Map: Outdoor Leisure 5 – The English Lakes North Eastern area; Landranger 80 – Penright, Keswick & Ambleside area.

Route:
Pooley Bridge (GR:471243)
The Cockpit (GR:492223)
High Street/Loadpot Hill (GR:457180)
High Howe (GR:467180)
Cockle Hill (GR:496196)
Heltondale (GR:503208)
Ketley Gate (GR:487224)
Pooley Bridge (GR:471243)

Nearest BR Station: Penrith.

Nearest Youth Hostel: Patterdale.

Approx Length: 14 miles (23km).

Time: Allow 3 hours.

Rating: Moderate. It is a long, steady climb up to Loadpot Hill at 671m; moreover, it can be difficult finding the way down.

This is a fine circular ride over the fells with magnificent views from Loadpot Hill. It links in with Rides 3 and 5, breaking down into three sections: a long ride up to the top of Loadpot Hill; a long downhill where navigation becomes tricky and a compass is necessary; and finally an easy ride back across Askham Fell.

1. Leave Pooley Bridge in the same direction as Ride 3, forking towards Howtown at the small church, crossing straight over at the crossroads, and following the dead-end road up past Howe Hill to the gate that leads out onto the fells. Persevere uphill on this track, and once again turn right at the bridleway crossroads for Howtown, forking left and then bearing right at The Cockpit.

2. A little further on you will see High Street going straight up to the left. This is the way you would go, except that what starts as a good track peters out to nothing and is lost amidst the moorland, only reasserting itself much further up the hill. Therefore keep on past High Street, and when you come to the ravine by the edge of Barton Park Woods look out for a track going off to the left just past it; this leads up the hillside.

3. Keep on up the main left hand track towards the top of Barton Fell, ignoring the narrower track which bears off to the right along the top of Long Crag with its steep face above Ullswater. Keep on the track which starts to bear south; eventually it comes up to Arthur's Pike, a distinctive rock outcrop on the right.

4. A little further on, go straight over at a crossing track, carrying on uphill. Still further on you come to High Street once again – by this stage a distinctive track once more – coming from the left. Bear right along it, going right and then left, steadily gaining height as you approach the top of Loadpot Hill (671m) with a trig point over to the left. From here the views are stupendous on a fine day.

6 A Tour of Grizedale Forest

Mainly Offroad

Area: The south-east Lake District. Start and finish from the car park at Grizedale Forest Centre.

OS Map: Outdoor Leisure 7 – The English Lakes South Eastern area; Landranger 96 – Barrow-in-Furness & South Lakeland area.

Route:
Grizedale Forest Centre CP (GR:335944)
Broad Piece/Blue Route (GR:331944)
China Plantation/Blue & Red junction (GR:335963)
Hawkshead Moor/Blue road junction (GR:343965)
Braithwaite Plantation/White Route (GR:342945)
Bogle Crag/Yellow Route (GR:343931)
Blind Lane/Yellow road junction (GR:346913)
Force Mills (GR:341911)
Satterthwaite (GR:339923)
Grizedale Forest Centre CP (GR:335944)

Nearest BR Station: Windermere.

Nearest Youth Hostel:
Hawkshead/Esthwaite Lodge.

Approx Length: 11 miles (18km).

Time: Allow 1–2 hours plus stops.

Rating: Easy. There are plenty of moderate ups and downs, but virtually all along clearly waymarked hard forest tracks.

This is an easy ride on forestry roads, ideal for those wanting an introduction to offroading, a family ride, or a training session (in which case you can try it three times round!). It uses half of the same route as Round Ennerdale (Ride 7), giving the option of extending the distance and difficulty.

1. Start from the Grizedale Forest Centre on the road between Hawkshead and Satterthwaite. This has a 'Forest Theatre', various displays, a large shop, and a highly original children's playground designed and made by a sculptor in wood. The Forestry Commission has marked out four cycle trails which are colour coded with very good signposting. Compared to real lakeland offroading they are all pretty tame since they run along hard-surfaced wide boulevards; but watch out for walkers and their dogs, who tend to spread across the way – even in full downhill flight it is important to slow down and be polite when passing. This route uses three of the official trails as well as a little roadwork and a bridleway to make a fast circuit which could take little more than an hour.

2. From the Forest Centre ride out onto the road, and then turn right down by the farm just past the postbox. Go past the large woodshed on the right, and there you will pick up the first of the blue route cycle track signposts taking you left over a cattle grid. Follow the signs uphill and round to the north, until after a couple of miles you come to red signs pointing left and blue pointing right. The red route heads up to High Cross, and is the way that Ride 7 follows en route to Hawkshead.

3. The blue cycle route leads to High Barn, where it joins the road. Turn right here. Ignore the first track to the left which is a footpath, and take the second which is marked by a white cycle route sign. This route will take you rapidly south down past the Forest Centre, until above Bogle Crag you pick up the first yellow cycle

route sign and turn left to follow it on what is probably the best part of the circuit for fast downhills.

4. The yellow route brings you down to the road at Blind Lane. Turn right here and then right again at Force Mills where there is a farmhouse tearoom on the corner. Follow the road up past a spectacular waterfall to Satterthwaite where there is a small pub and a post office, then ride on between the two tiny churches and look for a bridleway turning left on a right-hand bend. Go down the track here, following it past a children's playground and along the side of a stream. Go through a gate and follow the track ahead, bearing round to the right and going through another gate on the track which is far more offroad than those through the forestry.

5. Eventually the track comes to a T-junction at the bottom of the woods; turn right here (the other way goes to Coniston).

Further on the bridleway bears right off the track for a few hundred yards, but this is not at all obvious, and in fact by carrying on you soon rejoin the outward blue route and can head back down to the start point. Try getting round in under an hour...

and then drops do  
Tarn with distant  

4. Follow the har
keeping downhil
steeply down into
yard here is a sma
teas in the summer
good pub – the T 
tually next door to
Hill Top (NT), n

Places to Visit:
Grizedale Forest Centre.

Pubs and Cafés:
Café at Forest Centre;
pub nearby and at Satterthwaite;
tea room at Force Mills.

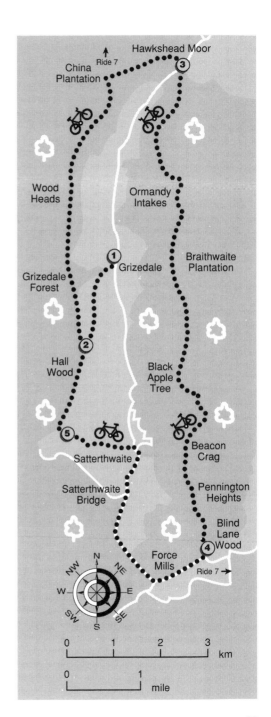

9 Over the Pennines

**Offroad and
On-Road**

Area: Cumbria. A tour across the North Pennines. Start and finish at Melmerby on the A686 to the north-east of Penrith, or at Kirkland about 5 miles (8km) due east of the A686 at Langwathby.

OS Map: Landrangers 91/87/86 – Appleby in Westmorland area/Hexham, Haltwhistle & surrounding area/ Haltwhistle, Bewcastle & Alston area.

Route:
Melmerby/A686 (GR:615373)
Kirkland (GR:645326)
Skirwith Fell (GR:700350)
Rotherhope Fell (GR:730400)
Garrigill (GR:745416)
Leadgate (GR:707438)
Melmerby/A686 (GR:615373)

Nearest BR Station:
Appleby-in-Westmorland.

Nearest Youth Hostel:
Alston or Dufton south along the Cumbria Cycleway from Kirkland.

Approx length: 26 miles (42km).

Time: Allow 4–5 hours.

Rating: Hard. Most of the old mining tracks are in pretty poor condition, and where the tracks fade out navigation can be tricky. There are two long climbs.

Mountain bike visitors to Cumbria flock to the Lake District, but seldom explore the country on the other side of the M6 motorway. Ten miles to the east of Penrith the Pennines rise dramatically in an uninterrupted chain. Here there is some wild country, with a handful of bridleways that traverse the Pennines. Compared with the summertime crowds in the Lakes you will find this is quiet country, with riding that is as tough, demanding and exhilarating as almost anywhere in the UK. The ride that follows gives a comparatively easy introduction to the area; two other routes are also suggested, but these are only for offroad hard riders.

1. Turn off the main A686 in Melmerby, and follow the minor road that leads south, keeping left through Row and Townhead. From there a track leads straight across to join the Cumbria Cycleway on the outskirts of Kirkland, a small hamlet at the foot of the Pennines where the roads stop, and wilderness starts. From here turn left up an avenue towards the Pennines, passing some picturesque holiday cottages and then going on to a rough track which begins to lead up the side of Kirkland Beck.

2. The going is almost immediately quite difficult, the route going fairly steeply uphill up on a loose surface; it levels out again for a while, but then climbs steeply again up the side of High Cap, weaving in and out of disused mine workings. Fine views soon open out behind, with the peaks of the Lakes clearly in view if the weather is clear.

3. Above the first set of mine workings care needs to be taken as the track appears to bend round to the left. This goes nowhere, and the unmarked bridleway route continues straight ahead by the side of a cairn over the moorland, with no more track and consequently some pretty demanding riding. Navigation here requires a mixture of compass and common sense. It is not a place to fool around on as the

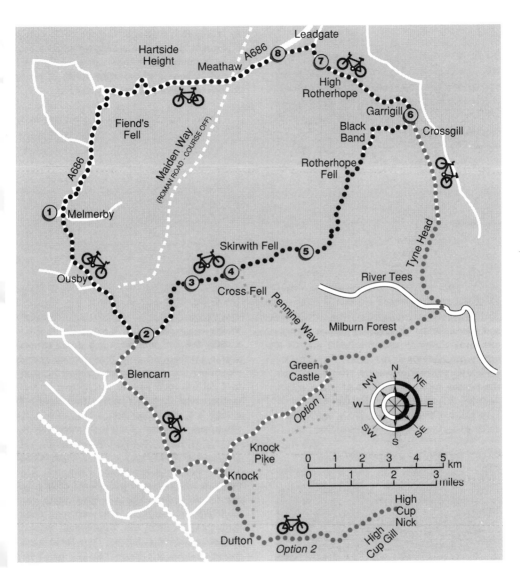

top is very exposed with no help to hand, and a great deal of hard rock to fall on. The high point of the ride at Cross Fell, where the trig point is at 893m, will frequently still have snow late into the spring.

4. Passing the screes beneath Cross Fell, the route once again joins a track which starts to head downhill. The track here is all that remains of a miners' road, though now the surface is only broken rock which requires good technical riding if you are to ride it all the way. A single tin hut on the way up is the only building on this bleak moorland landscape until you come to a battered slate building which now acts as a bothy. The door is always open,

The Yorkshire Dales

The Yorkshire Dales offer some of the best offroad cycling in Britain, with a tremendous variety of old roads, tracks and trails crossing the high hills and dales. The northern part of the dales is particularly well served with offroad routes that are for the most part on hard ground and offer fast riding as they cut though the unforgiving terrain. The uphill riding can be tough, but the downhills sometimes seem to go on forever. Note that much of the high riding is also very exposed, and care should be taken accordingly; when the landscape is lost from sight in murk and rain it may be better to postpone your ride until the weather and the views get better. Only go if you are sure of your capabilities.

Ride 10: Grassington, Mastiles Lane and Malham Tarn

Ride 11: Round Nidderdale via Scar House Reservoir

Ride 12: Langstrothdale Chase and the Cam High Road

Ride 13: Gunnerside Gill in Swaledale

Ride 14: Gunnerside and Kisdon Force

Ride 15: North of Reeth in Swaledale

Ride 16: South of Reeth in Swaledale

Ride 17: Marske in Swaledale

Ride 18: North of Swaledale and Barningham Moor

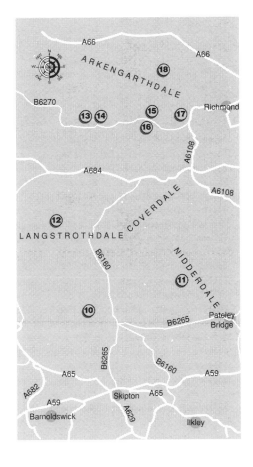

Malham Cove is one of nature's finest creations in the Dales. Park your bike and explore it!

Cycleway. Go straight ahead, following the road due west with Malham Tarn coming into sight on the right – this is the second largest expanse of open water in Yorkshire. Near Tarn Foot you cross a stream that helps feed the tarn, and a little further on you will see a bridleway sign by a gate set in the fence on the left.

6. Go through here, and follow the bridleway posts up the hillock; the footpath goes round to the left. Follow the bridleway on up and over the top, with the posts clearly showing the way across Dean Moor, going through a gate set in a wall and riding down and up to join the road at Langscar Gate. Turn left onto the road, which is a magnificent downhill into the village of Malham, weaving down through the bends at top speed with the might of Malham Cove over to the left; its sooty streaks of lichen are said to have been the inspiration for Tom the chimney sweep in Charles Kingsley's 'Water Babies', and if you feel inclined it is well worth stopping and making a closer inspection on foot, walking up the track by the side of the cove which leads to the incredible limestone pavement at the top.

7. A little further on the road goes sharp left on a bend where there's a bridleway sign pointing straight ahead. If you want to go down into Malham off road, this is the way, following an old but easily ridable track called Long Lane that heads downhill between the fields, bearing left at the bottom to bring you out near the car park and information centre. Malham itself is a tidy little place with a few shops, cafés and a pub, and can be very popular with tourists, trippers and walkers. We found a really excellent place for tea at the bottom of Cove Road which leads down from Malham Tarn, a small hotel with outside tables set by the side of a small stream.

8. Malham is about halfway along the route. To continue the ride turn left in the centre of Malham, following a dead-end road that heads north-east past Gordale Bridge and Gordale House. You come steeply downhill to the bridge, and here you might care to jump off and investigate the local sights which include the waterfall named Janet's Foss to the right, and Gordale Scar, a magnificent fissure in the hillside which is about a $^1/_3$ mile (0.5km) off to the left. Carry on up the lane, which changes from Gordale Lane to Hawthorne Lane (although nobody would notice). It is all fairly steep uphill, but the views get better better and you are unlikely to meet much motorized traffic.

9. After a good climb turn off to the right at the first bridleway sign you come to. Follow the track which runs uphill to a gate by a trig point; here the bridleway splits, going south towards Calton and south-east towards Hetton. The latter is the way to go. At first there is some kind of track through the grass, but this soon peters out into a maze of tracks and ditches as you head across Hetton Common. The riding is not too bad, but the way is by no means obvious. Keep quite well to the left, passing by a solitary farm building and making roughly towards the left corner of the Winterburn Reservoir ahead. The trick is to cross the ravine at Ray Gill close by the farm building, and then follow its far side down towards the northern end of the reservoir in a south-westerly direction – if you are on the west side of this ravine, which gets deeper and deeper, you're on the wrong side.

Fine country looking out from Grassington, with the drystone walls marking out the fields.

10. After a time you hit a trail which brings you down by the side of a few trees at Whetstone Gill (not the woods shown on the OS map), joining a track that runs north from High Gill farmhouse by the side of the reservoir. Turn left and then right here, crossing the old bridge over the stream (Hetton Common Beck) which feeds the reservoir, and following the rough track which bears right up the hill on a rough track on the far side. Keep on up in the same direction, crossing open moorland until you come to a five-way signpost by a gate set in a wall. This shows the footpaths and bridleways that radiate from this point; go through the gate following the sign for Hetton, which takes you there via Moor Lane – a long, straight and very fast track running between old walls on a slight downhill.

11. Where this track meets the road in Hetton there is a pub just up to the left, which appears to be a popular place for dinner and will just about accept a muddy biker. To continue, turn left along the road, once again following the Yorkshire Dales Cycleway towards Cracoe; you are told it is the Yorkshire Dales Cycleway on the OS map, but I never saw any signs on these roads. Follow this minor road from Hetton across the railway, joining the B6265 just before you come to Cracoe. Past this junction there is a clearly signposted bridleway going off to the left by the side of a house.

12. Follow this track (Swinden Lane) under the railway bridge, turning right and left along the side of fields. Turn right with the track again, and then go through a gate and across a couple of grass fields, passing a disused building on the way. With the immense Swinden Quarry grinding and bumping over to the right, this brings you to a patch of trees with a dip into a small ravine to cross the Eller Beck beyond. Cross over, and bear right up the other side, picking your way across the grass in a north-east direction. The track is marked by bridleway posts, and you link up with a proper track (yet another Moor Lane) that leads you rapidly down to the B62675 which is here called Tarns Lane.

13. Go straight over, joining the bridleway track on the other side, going steeply uphill, levelling out with fields either side, and then heading down to the road (Lauderdale Lane) just outside Linton. This is a really picturesque little place with a pub in a fantastic setting; there is

Mastiles Lane gives a fine offroad ride from Conistone to Malham Tarn with just a few steady hills.

also a youth hostel here. Ride through Linton and then bear right off the road up a narrow lane. This leads you out onto the B6160 where you bear right again, passing the school buildings and following another part of the Yorkshire Dales Cycleway. (Alternatively, if you have had enough, turn left along the B6160 and follow the road direct to Grassington, which is across the valley.)

14. Keep on for a mile or so past a lane that bears off to the right, and at the next right turn go left through a gate going offroad once again on bridleway. Ride along with the old wall on your right, passing through the next gate and then heading on a fast downhill across the field beyond – again keep over to the right away from the woods. When the quaint little suspension bridge comes into view in the valley, head down towards it.

15. This bridge is a wonderful construction, built by a local man in the nineteenth century. It is only one person wide, and carrying a bike across is so tricky that if the water is down you would do better using the stepping stones across the River Wharfe; if you do use the bridge, be careful not to get in the way of pedestrians. On the other side the river bank is a pleasant place to stop and rest awhile, before going through the gate ahead and riding along the edge of the next field which brings you to a quiet lane by Mill Bridge. Turn left here up through Hebden

(where there is another pub), crossing straight over the road and continuing on a lane ahead.

16. This soon turns into a tarmac bridleway/footpath following by the side of the stream called Hebden Beck, leading north towards the few houses at Hole Bottom, where you go through another gate leaving tarmac and civilization behind. Here you join a track which follows the right side of Hebden Beck – follow it along by the side of the beck, and some way on it switches to the left side, going up and downhill and coming to a track which zig-zags up the hillside to the left. This is just past an isolated ruined house (old mine workings) on the right – the track that carries on ahead by the side of the beck soon peters out.

17. Follow the zig-zags up to the left until you come to a gateway. Go through here and carry on straight ahead, passing old mine workings on the left with a number of labelled educational signposts telling you how things used to be – you might expect to see the occasional school parties here. Keep on the wide track which bears round to the left, heading due west until it hits the road by the fine old house at Yarnbury. Here you turn left down another 'Moor Lane', and soon commence a very fast downhill into Grassington – a brilliant end to a brilliant ride.

Places to Visit:
Malham Tarn, Malham Cove, Gordale Scar;
National Park Information Centres at Malham and Grassington;
Kilnsey Park Trout Farm (tel: 01756 752224) at Kilnsey Park.

Pubs and Cafés:
Pubs in Grassington and Malham; pubs also at Kilnsey, Hetton and Linton. Cafés and shops in Grassington and Malham.

11 Round Nidderdale via Scar House Reservoir

Offroad and On-Road

Area: The south of the Yorkshire Dales. Start and finish at Pateley Bridge on B6265 north-west of Harrogate. Car parking available.

OS Map: OS Outdoor Leisure 30 – Yorkshire Dales Northern & Central areas; OS Landranger 99 – Northallerton, Ripon & surrounding area.

Route:
Pateley Bridge (GR:159656)
Gouthwaite Reservoir/Nidderdale Way (GR:130688)
Ramsgill (GR:118711)
Lofthouse (GR:101733)
Middlesmoor (GR:092740)
Sar House Reservoir/Nidderdale Way (GR:068766)
North Moor (GR:079778)
Bracken Ridge (GR:110768)
Ouster Bank (GR:120748)
Summer Edge (GR:141748)
Bouthwaite (GR:123712)
Wath (GR:149678)
Pateley Bridge (GR:159656)

Nearest BR Station: No station within easy reach.

Nearest Youth Hostel: Linton on B6265 west of Pateley Bridge.

Approx Length: 28 miles (45km).

Time: Allow 4 hours plus stops.

Rating: A reasonably energetic ride. It's a very long uphill from Lofthouse to Middlesmoor, and there are a few tricky sections when riding offroad.

This is a great ride following the ridges above both sides of the Nidderdale valley, with two fine offroad sections leading to and from the Scar House Reservoir. Pateley Bridge, a pleasant, small town on the edge of the Yorkshire Dales, is the start point for the full ride which divides into three separate circuits which could also be started from Lofthouse or the Scar House Reservoir car park with the option of cutting out one or more circuits to reduce the distance.

1. From the car park in Pateley Bridge head down the hill and across the bridge over the River Nidd. Take the first right turning by a garage, following the road signposted to Lofthouse and Middlemoor along Nidderdale. This is a pleasant up and down country road without too much traffic. For a couple of miles it follows the side of the Gouthwaite Reservoir, passing Ramsgill with its solitary pub and the village of Lofthouse.

2. A little way on a short diversion to the left brings you to How Stean Gorge, which is well worth investigating with interesting caves and a walkway cut into the side of the Gorge. The How Stean Gorge Café is open every day, and serves really excellent food including its famous roast Nidderdale beef and Yorkshire pudding. If you want to start from here, there's a small car park down by the bridge that crosses How Stean Beck (GR:097733).

3. From here carry on up the road, starting the long uphill to Middlesmoor. This gets steeper and steeper and is a hard climb, sweeping round a right hand bend with the small church of this hamlet above you. Once you have arrived, this little place is worth a walk round, and has a well-sited pub with a view over the hillside if you are ready for refreshment. To continue ride on up through the hamlet. Beyond the houses the road turns into a track called Moor Lane. At first the surface is pretty good, but it deteriorates as you get higher.

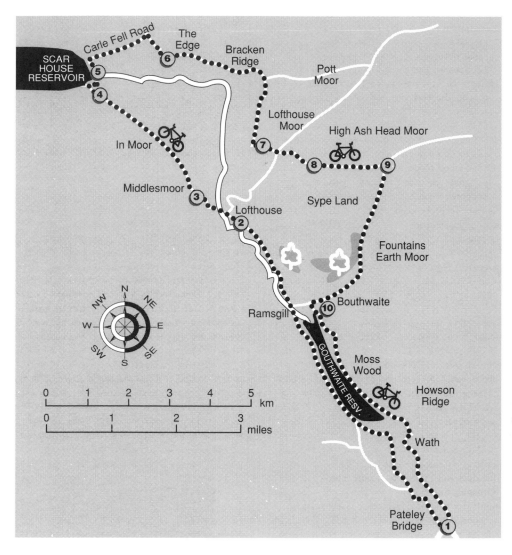

4. Once on top of the moor there are fine views on either side, and except for opening and closing gates it is a fast track all the way until you reach the steep downhill to Scar House Reservoir, which lies in the next valley. The track snakes right and left down the hillside here, with most of the surface eroded and rocky, thus demanding some expertise. Below lies the enormous reservoir with its fine dam; once down there you can sprint across the dam and bear left on a track going uphill on the other side.

5. After about 75 yards is a bridleway sign indicating a right turn onto the Carle Fell Road track; follow this on a gradual uphill. Some of the going may be boggy. After a while the track sweeps down to the left to cross Woo Gill with a

steep uphill on the far side – this is your first technical ascent, and riding the short way to the top without putting a foot down is difficult. After another rather easier up and down, the track carries on past a remote shooting house where in the shooting season there could be guns around.

6. The bridleway swings north and south and needs to be followed carefully, before it follows a good track along the contours of Dale Edge which gives an excellent, high speed ridge ride with some spectacular views over the surrounding landscape in clear weather. Having passed across Masham Moor the track bears right past Lofthouse Moor, until you eventually come to a second shooting house – they are really no more than crudely built brick huts – just above Thrope Edge.

7. A short way on from here bear off to the left, following the track down to Moor High Road. If you turn right this leads downhill along Trapping Hill to Lofthouse which is a quick way to finish the ride or visit the pub, but for a further offroad section turn left and then right after no more than 100 yards, passing through a gate to follow a track across Fountains Earth Moor.

8. When the track forks, take the left fork heading on a fast surface due east – on the map this does not appear to be the shortest way to Ramsgill, but it gives the best riding. To the south you will see a couple of unusually shaped rocks known as Jenny Twigg and Her Daughter Tib: some way on you take a sharp right turn marked by a boulder set in the side of the track.

9. This brings you downhill south on a very fast track, rejoining the other track near an old bridge, and then carrying on steeply downhill through trees until you reach a lane. By this stage you should be ready for a pub. To find the nearest, ride on straight ahead until you rejoin the Pateley Bridge–Middlesmoor Road, turning left for a short way to reach the York Arms at

Typical Dales scenery via an old road. Some of these routes are now threatened by 4WD destruction.

Ramsgill, which is a pleasant and rather smart pub in a fine village green situation. The ride this far from Pateley Bridge is likely to take at least three hours.

10. To continue, retrace your wheeltracks back along the lane northwards, turning right onto a lane which heads along the north side of Gouthwaite Reservoir. This soon turns to a bridleway track, following the edge of the reservoir with a few ups and downs and a little mud in wet weather, passing high above the fine Victorian dam at its south-east end, and then heading downhill on a steep track to emerge by a lodge. Here you turn left on the road which leads back to Pateley Bridge. An hour or so's riding from Ramsgill should see you back at Pateley, hopefully in time for tea.

Places to Visit:
The Nidderdale Museum at Pateley which has has an Information Centre, cafés and shops;
How Stean Gorge near Lofthouse;
Yorkshire Country Wines (tel: 01423 711947) at Glasshouses near Pateley Bridge.

Pubs and Cafés:
Pubs in Pateley Bridge;
pubs also at Ramsgill, Lofthouse and Middlesmoor.

---

13 Gunnerside Gill

**Offroad and
On-Road**

Area: Gunnerside, Swaledale, Yorkshire
Dales. Start and finish at Gunnerside;
limited parking available.

OS Map: Outdoor Lesiure 30 –
Yorkshire Dales Northern & Central
area; Landranger 98/92 – Wensleydale &
Upper Wharfedale/Barnard Castle &
surrounding area.

Route:
Gunnerside (GR:951982)
Feetham/B6270 via bridleway
(GR:987984)
Surrender Bridge (GR:987999)
Surrender Ground/Great Pinseat
(GR:970024)
Fincher Gill/Level House (GR:963014)
Blakethwaite Dams/Gunnerside Moor
(GR:936030)
Botcher Gill Nook/Lownathwaite
(GR:935006)
Jingle Pot Edge (GR:940993)
Dyke Heads (GR:941983)
Gunnerside (GR:951982)

Nearest BR Station: Knaresborough.

Nearest Youth Hostels:
Keld or Grinton.

Approx Length: 15 miles (24km).

Time: Allow 3 hours.

Rating: Moderate. There are stiff
climbs to be tackled out of Gunnerside
and Feetham. The tracks are mainly
across rocky moorland. The bridleway
turning away from Melbecks Moor up
Gunnerside Gill is easily missed.

*This is a good ride made great by very
good riding and spectacular views down
Gunnerside Gill, but be prepared for lots of
climbing! In Gunnerside you can park by
the wall on a dead-end lane going north,
just over the bridge from the pub. The
route can be conveniently combined with
the companion Ride 14 out of Gunnerside
which it crosses at Dyke Heads.*

1. Ride through Gunnerside in the direction
of Reeth, and just past the last house on the
right turn off onto the track which goes steeply
up to the left. Follow it uphill, and where it
bends left continue straight ahead on a rougher
track past the back of a farm building. Follow
this track due east, steadily gaining height up
the hillside – it is easy to follow, but quite hard
riding. After a while you will see the farm building at Heights ahead with a barn on the hillside
above you. Bear left round the back of Heights
on the grassy track which continues past Shake
Holes shown on the map until the track
becomes tarmac.

2. Carry on along this track with good views
across the valley, dropping down past the attractive cluster of houses at Blades. From here the
track drops rapidly down to Feetham where it
rejoins the B6270 road. Bear left past the
hotel/pub, or stop there for sustenance for the
hill ahead, and take the next road turning to the
left uphill signposted for Langthwaite. Grind on
up past Le Routier at Peat Gate Head, gradually
gaining height on the road as you pass the farm
at Gallows Top over to the right.

3. Pass a footpath sign to the left and then
head downhill for Surrender Bridge. Cross over,
and ignore the first bridleway sign to the left, or
take it if you want to make the route shorter on
a better surface than the top track offers. Continue uphill on the road, and after about half a
mile you will see a track to the left with a second
bridleway sign.

4. Head offroad here, steadily gaining height

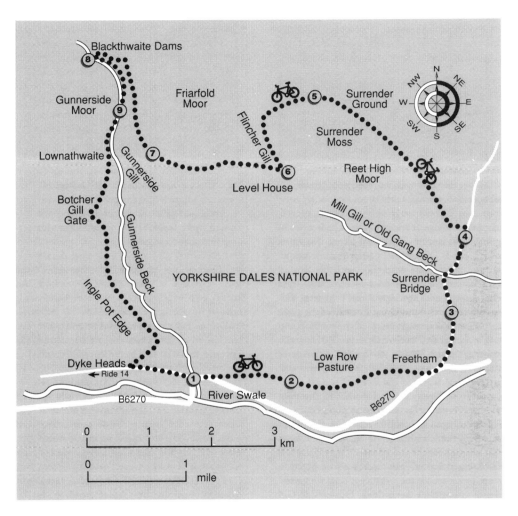

on an easy uphill. Keep on the track, which is easily followed on level ground, but of variable quality, passing over a couple of boggy sections. Keep straight on, heading for the tips ahead which are marked by a conspicuous pair of cairns with posts in. When you reach the cairns bear left to head for the next single cairn through old mine workings. The track becomes somewhat vague here; just bear left riding parallel with the wall on your right, heading downhill and towards the line of mine workings, which leave a long scar up the hill on the far side of the valley.

5. The track heads down and then bears left through a gate, entering another area of mine workings at the spot marked Ford. Keep left here; the track goes down and up, and you should ignore another track which appears to go off to the right. Some way on you pass a ruined mine building just below Level House, where the track improves; take the track going off to the right here, well before you come to the next gate.

6. The new track leads uphill along Old Rake Hush, passing a crossing bridle track to the

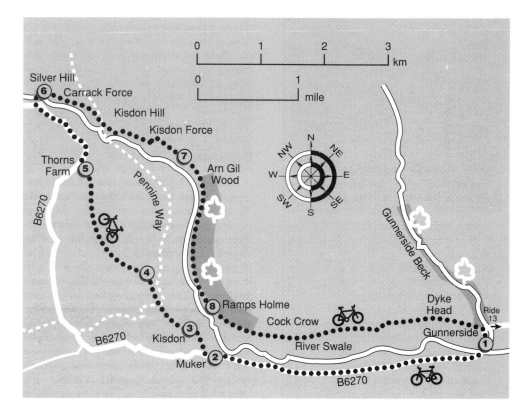

up with a wall on the left – all but a few true heroes will have to push this section! The track remains easy to follow as it levels out and bears left through a gate before leaving the stone walls behind. Head downhill across grass to the next gate set in a wall by a sheepfold, going through and bearing right downhill on the hard grassy surface with more fine views to the left. Keep on down this hill on the easily followed track which starts to turn rubbly and becomes tricky to ride near the bottom, by which time your descent has already been slowed by several gates. From here the track bears left across a ford at Skeb Skeugh, before heading uphill and joining the road by Thorns Farm.

5. Turn right along the road, ignoring the two signs for 'Keld only' as you pass the war memorial, and a little further on turn right over Park

Bridge; from here you get a fine view of Wain Wath Force waterfalls upstream which is a popular picnic spot and no doubt at its most dramatic in winter. Over the bridge the road bears right uphill. Where it bends left go straight ahead through a gate and onto a track signposted to East Stonesdale Farm.

6. The track goes left downhill past Carrack Force waterfalls, and then bears uphill to the right. After passing through several gates it comes down to East Stonesdale Farm where you turn right with the farmhouse on your right and a barn on your left, going through a gate and then steeply downhill on a rocky track. This bears left down to the magnificent waterfalls at Kisdon Force in a fine setting which is perfect for a rest stop, although it is likely to be popular as it lies along the Pennine Way.

Shut all gates whenever you pass through, and have respect for the land, its people and animals.

7. Follow the track through a gate above the falls and continue along it uphill, bearing left and right and following the course of the River Swale in a most beautiful setting. Ignore the track off to the left which goes up to Crackpot Hall, and you soon follow the track downhill to the footbridge and ford at Fair Yew End at a curve in the river. From here the track drops down to follow level ground by the side of the river, and gives splendid easy riding. Follow the bridle track past the woods on your left and on through a gate with Ramps Holme Bridge ahead. When the track divides before the bridge, take the main track uphill to the left while walkers take the narrower track ahead.

8. As the track climbs above Ramps Holme Farm a sign informs you that 'the road' bears left. This is a tarmac track which plugs uphill with the occasional down, steadily gaining height on the hillside as it heads east past Calvert Houses and Ivelet Heads. At Gunnerside Lodge it heads down to the right where it meets a T-junction. Turn left down to the bridge here, following the road round to the right uphill past Shoregill Head and then on past the houses at Dyke Heads from where it is the same fast descent into Gunnerside as in Ride 13.

Waterfalls are at their best after a period of heavy rain. You may get muddy but it's worth it!

Places to Visit:
Wain Wath and Kisdon Force waterfalls.

Pubs and Cafés:
Pub in Reeth;
pub and teashop in Muker.

Two cairns mark the route on the heights above Strothwaite Hall. If they fall down, help to rebuild them!

6. From Langthwaite go over the bridge, and then left onto the road signposted for Reeth. Head along this road through the small hamlet of Arkle Town where the road crosses the Fore Gill stream and then goes uphill. Just past the cattle grid a bridleway sign indicates a grassy track turning right onto Reeth Low Moor. Ride along this track, keeping right as it heads gradually uphill, though not enough to be hard going. After a time the track levels out, and then bears right and heads slightly downhill towards a conspicuous tip on the hillside ahead.

7. Bear off to the left here about 100 yards before these mine tips, taking a grassy track which heads up between Calver Hill and Cringley Hill. The track comes and goes with some riding on grass and some on heather, but the going is not too bad and you soon come round the side of Calver Hill and begin to head downhill, still following what there is of a track in a more or less direct line.

8. Carry straight over at a grass crossing track near to a corrugated iron shack, and then bear downhill to the right, taking the shortest possible route through the heather to join the conspicuous track ahead which runs along the side of a wall. Turn left onto this hard track and head downhill above the farm building named Nova Scotia, but just before you reach the next farm building named Thirns, turn hard right onto a track which takes you back towards Nova Scotia.

9. About 25 yards from Nova Scotia bear left downhill on a grassy track which runs down the left side of a wall. Follow the track down on a fast and very enjoyable descent towards woods, going through a gate at the bottom, and then straight up the short hill ahead and out through a narrow bridleway gate. From here turn left past Thirnswood Hall and follow the tarmac drive down to a minor road. Turn left and rejoin the B6270 at Helaugh, from where it is about 1 1/2 miles (2.5km) back along the road into Reeth.

Places to Visit:
The Swaledale Folk Museum at Reeth which also has an Information Centre.

Pubs and Cafés:
Pubs and cafés in Reeth; pub in Langthwaite.

16 South of Reeth

Area: Reeth, Swaledale, Yorkshire Dales. Start and finish at Reeth; roadside parking available.

OS Map: Outdoor Leisure 30 – Yorkshire Dales Northern & Central area; Landranger 98 – Wensleydale & Upper Wharfedale.

Route:
Reeth (GR:037993)
Reeth Bridge/Low Fremington (GR:045990)
Grinton (GR:047983)
Ridley Hush (GR:038963)
Dent's House (GR:031942)
Apedale Road (GR:020945)
Morley's Folly/Whitaside Moor (GR:993956)
Beldow Hill (GR:006972)
Shot Pot (GR:013978)
Stubbin Farm (GR:019984)
How Hill (GR:031986)
Grinton (GR:047983)
Reeth Bridge/Low Fremington (GR:045990)
Reeth (GR:037993)

Nearest BR station: Knaresborough.

Nearest Youth Hostel: Grinton Lodge.

Approx length: 14^{1}/$_{2}$ miles (23km).

Time: Allow 3 hours.

Rating: Moderate. There is a long climb on road from Grinton to Ridley Hush; then rough miners' tracks and narrow moorland tracks through heather; and the last section along river, which could be very muddy. Careful navigation is needed on moorland section beyond Morley's Folly.

After the ride north of Reeth (Ride 15) you will want more; this makes a suitable complementary ride, and both can easily be completed in a day with a good break for lunch in between. Its attractions include good technical riding through heather, a fast descent from the moor, and a good riverside ride to finish.

1. Head downhill out of Reeth on the B6270 once again, crossing the bridge and continuing past Fremington. After crossing the next bridge over the Swale keep straight ahead through Grinton, up the hill on the road for Bellerby and Castle Bolton. Press on uphill, and when the country starts to open out take the next right turning signposted to Castle Bolton. (Turn left for the youth hostel which is very close to here at Grinton Lodge.)

2. There follows a long and quite hard uphill, with moorland on either side. Every time you think you are near the top you find there is still more climbing ahead of you! About 2^{1}/$_{2}$ miles (4km) from Reeth there is a straight level section which crosses a stream called Ridley Hush where the ground has been badly eroded by the force of the water – it is an easily spotted landmark. On the right is a bridleway sign pointing out across the moor, and in the far distance you can see two cairns on the top of a hill: head for these.

3. Leave the road and follow the bridleway sign's general direction on a track which comes and goes through disused mineworks, but is easily followed and is not too strenuous. The track eventually heads steeply up to the two cairns, with a fence running across beyond. Turn left along the fence and ride along to another fence where you go through a gate, following the clear, hard and very bumpy track which takes you south on a fast downhill towards Dent's Houses. You will know you are there when you see a barn on the left, a track going on ahead up the hill past a lonely building, and the Apedale Road turning right, which is the route that you take.

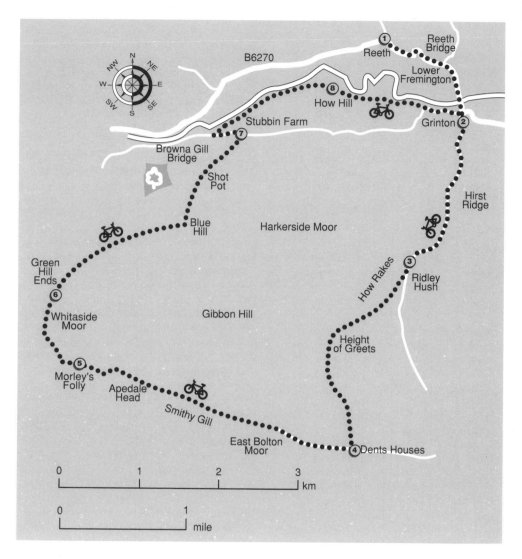

4. At first this is a good fast track. However, after about 1 mile (1.5km) there's a tricky technical uphill on loose gravel, and then the track becomes less obvious as it passes a lonely railway carriage and heads on into the wilderness. The track bears left and goes through a gateway in a fence past a large crater, before bearing right and following a wiggly course over strange ground disfigured by mineworkings. You pass Morley's Folly with the remains of a small building on a hillock to the left, and then come down to a pile of shale by a cairn with a pole stuck in it.

5. Turn right – due north – here on a shale track which becomes grassy and enters a gully after about 100 yards, heading down past grouse butts looking like mini turrets. A short

The old road along Smithy Gill is there care of the people who once laboured in the area.

Take your time on a ride of this kind. Check the map and the scenery, and take some photos!

way on the track continues north out of the gully, and heads along a narrow track through the heather which is interspersed by grassy sections. The riding from here on is technical but good fun!

6. A cairn over to the left indicates another bridleway heading down to the road at Sheepfold. You keep to the right, following the track round to the east with fine views over Swaledale as you negotiate the way past a large crater. Continue on the track, which becomes easier to ride as it heads down to a lonely footbridge. Cross this bridge, and ride on past the back of a timber building. Ignore the track off to the right, and follow the more obvious track which starts a fast winding descent, bringing you down to the road above Stubbin Farm in record time.

7. Turn left down the hill here, and after a couple of hundred yards take the bridleway to the right signposted to Grinton. This starts on a grassy track which heads downhill, and then follows a stone wall before dropping down to the river. From there on you have an excellent riverside ride along the Swale, though in some places the bank has been washed away by floodwater and carrying becomes necessary. Go through several bridleway gates/stiles which are all marked with blue blobs, continuing along the riverside until the river bends left and you come to the end of the trees.

8. Here, head diagonally right across an open field, going through a gate on the far right hand side where you turn immediately right and left onto a well-worn track. This bears right uphill through a gate, and then keeps to the left along the side of trees, going through another gate and continuing in a more or less easterly direction. The track remains easy to follow, passing through several more gates on a variable surface and passing below a couple of farm buildings Eventually it comes alongside the Swale for one last time, and then rejoins the road on a bend by Swale Hall. Turn left here and ride along the road to Grinton, passing the church and taking the next left back to Reeth.

Places to Visit:
Swaledale Folk Museum in Reeth where there is also an Information Centre.

Pubs and Cafés:
Pubs and cafés in Reeth.

---

17 Marske in Swaledale

On-Road and Offroad

Area: Swaledale, Yorkshire Dales. Start and finish at Marske; limited parking near post office.

OS Map: Outdoor Leisure 30 – Yorkshire Dales Northern & Central areas; Landranger 92/99 – Barnard Castle/ Northallerton, Ripon & surrounding area.

Route:
Marske (GR:105005)
Sour Nook (GR:109992)
Low Oxque (GR:101986)
Crook Bank Lane (GR:071989)
Helwith Road (GR:070009)
Skelton Moor (GR:077022)
Orgate Bridge (GR:092017)
Marske (GR:105005)

Nearest BR Station: Northallerton.

Nearest Youth Hostel: Grinton Lodge near Grinton.

Approx Length: 10 miles (16km).

Time: Allow 2–3 hours.

Rating: Moderate. There is one hard climb; mainly hard tracks; some overgrown sections; and some that could be muddy. Care is needed to find the bridleway route from Low Oxque to Shaw Bank.

This route is conveniently close to the two circuits out of Reeth (Rides 15 and 16), and offers fine views with plenty of variety in a short ride. Start from Marske by the post office where there is limited parking on the roadside.

1.   Ride downhill, and then bear left and uphill past Marske Hall, which looks fairly splendid. Ride on up the road which bends right and then starts a long downhill towards the River Swale.

2.   Ignore the first bridleway sign on the right, and turn off the road at the second bridleway sign about 50 yards further down the hill – it is on a left-hand bend close to the river, about 1 mile (1½km) from Marske. Ride along a good track with this beautiful river on your left. The track takes you past the woods at Oxque Bridge and you soon come to the farmstead at Low Oxque.

3.   Here the bridleway turn is easy to miss, turning right on an indistinct track uphill towards old disused farm buildings, well before you reach the farmhouse and its modern barns. When I rode up the way was also very overgrown, and it may be easier riding during a hard spell in winter. Keep on up the hill heading ENE, going over an old gate which takes you onto a track that is in a poor state but improves as you gain height.

4.   After a time High Oxque farmhouse comes into sight ahead. Before the gate the bridleway bears left round the side of the hill on an old indistinct track, leaving the more obvious track which runs down to the farmhouse. This brings you up to the top of Shaw Bank with fine views over to the north. Ride alongside a stone wall on top of the world, and when you are well past High Oxque bear downhill on a track which leads back down to join up with the farmhouse track in the valley. This track down is easily missed.

5.   Keep along the track and through a few

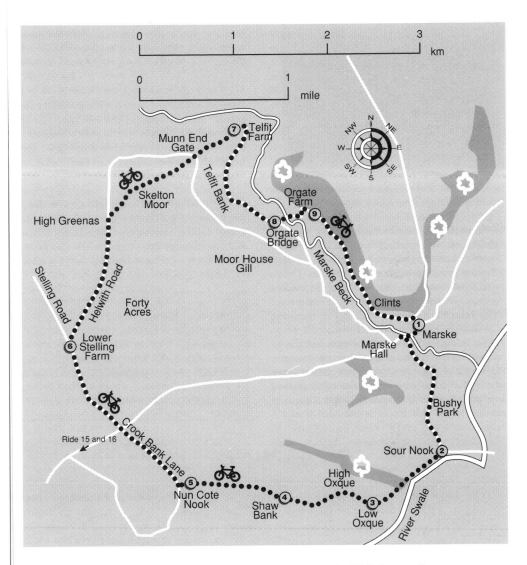

gates till you come out onto Crook Bank Lane by Nun Cote Nook farmstead. From here you can turn left to the White Horse at Marrick if you feel in need of refreshment. If not, turn right and ride along this straight road which soon leads up to a crossroads. Cross over and carry straight on, passing the driveway to Lower Stelling Farm. A few hundred yards further on Helwith Road leads clearly off to the right with

a signpost for High Greenas Farm.

6. This is a very fast downhill on a tarmac track which becomes greener as it heads towards the moor; it then goes uphill to join a crossing track with High Greenas Farm off to the left. Turn right through the gate here, and then bear diagonally left across the open moorland, following the clearly defined track. You

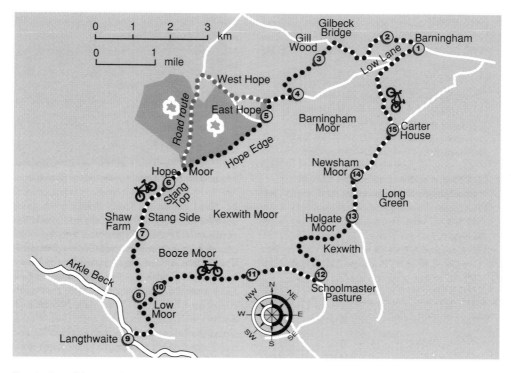

Barningham Moor at Cowclose Gill. From here there is no semblance of a track, and riding over the moorland grass is hard going. Head more or less straight uphill, and then bear along the right side of a ravine which soon brings you to a hard crossing track running down from Haythwaite farmstead. Following this through East Hope and West Hope to the road beyond is a worthwhile option is you do not fancy picking your way through the forest as decribed below.

5. Turn right along this track into the woods to link up with the Forestry bridleway. Shortly after the track enters the woods, take a left turn before Drydale Gill and head south. From here keep more or less south-west. The correct route should bring you out on the Stang Road just beyond the forestry, but with a confusing mass of forestry tracks and the bridleway obliterated the best I could do was emerge on a track which hit the road some way down the hill after a lot of riding over hard shale, mainly uphill. The object is then to get to the top of the hill, past

the forestry and into open moorland.

6. At Stang Top you will pass the County Durham/North Yorkshire border sign. The road from there on is as pleasant as any you will cycle on, taking you on a long and a very fast downhill with great scenery on both sides. About a mile from the forestry you pass Stang House over to the right by a pond, and some way on Shaw Farm on the same side of the road next to a conspicuous bridge crossing Shaw Beck. A few hundred yards further on you will see a bridleway sign pointing off to the left up a well defined track which is where you turn offroad.

7. Head uphill on the track which bends round to the left and then the right as it gains height, winding its way past the rock face below Windegg-Vein which appears to be a popular place for climbing. The track continues past mine workings and tips, and then doubles back in a U-bend to the left. Ignore this bend and keep straight on, heading south on a much less

well defined track. Keep your course and it will eventually bring you down to a stone wall by Peat Moor Green.

8. Go through the metal gate here, and then ride down the field by the left hand wall where a gully marks the bridleway track. At the bottom go through another gate, and then head left down the gully, which continues bearing east-south-east – it was once a walled track, but the walls have fallen in and this short section is consequently mainly unridable. It brings you down to a gate by a ruined building with a farmstead up the hill to the left.

9. Here turn right down Scotty Hill, following the track round to the right past a few buildings and then on a steeper downhill into Langthwaite. This is a picture postcard place with an incredibly narrow main street, single village store, and the Red Lion pub where you can sit outside and enjoy the food. The ride thus far is about 11^{1}/$_{2}$ miles (18.5km).

10. From Langthwaite retrace your route back up the hill, rejoining the track onto Peat Moor Green. This time when you reach the U-bend by the tips, bear right uphill through the old mine workings. The track soon bends round to the west, heading past a gully towards a wooden building. Keep on past this building until you come to a clear right-hand turning after a few hundred yards. This drops you back down onto the bridleway route which was lost in the heather, bearing left on a track which continues as good, fast riding. You will see the Stony Man boundary stone on your right, and then the Moresdale Road continues downhill across the fine open spaces of Kexwith Moor.

11. When you reach some grouse butts look over to the left – you will see the farm buildings at Kexwith, and the track going up the hill behind them is the route you are making for. Keep on past the grouse butts until the present track reaches a stone wall with farm buildings at Schoolmaster Pasture some way ahead.

12. Bear left around this wall on a much less well-defined track which heads north and then swings north-west along the left side of a wall. When you are opposite the barn on the hill above Kexwith, ride by the first gate set at right angles in the wall and look for the second gate which is about 200 yards further on.

13. Go through, and follow the track downhill and over the stream. Ride up to the farm buildings and cross the bridge, going past a modern barn and bearing left on the track which takes you up the hillside. This track bears right and left before going through a gate, taking you across Holgate Moor on a good surface until it reaches a minor road ahead.

14. Turn left on the road on a fast downhill. The road then bears right and uphill, passing a cattle grid by the entrance to Long Green Farm with its large buildings over to the right. Less than a mile further on you pass Byers Hill Farm away to the left, after which the road goes down and up, levelling out past a small disused quarry. Ride past the next field, looking for a gateway on the left with a track running down the right hand side of the field past a couple of old barns at Carter House. This half-mile track is not a bridleway or footpath, but a sign indicates that it is used by walkers and it is the only way of connecting with the bridleway ahead.

15. Go through the next gate and follow the track which is now bridleway round to the right. It is easy to follow as it winds mainly downhill, crossing a ford by a footbridge and then bearing left towards buildings. Cross the cattle grid and join the road, riding down the hill ahead which soon brings you to the green at Barningham, hopefully in time to try the pub.

Places to Visit:
Swaledale Folk Museum at Reeth; Bowes Museum and Barnard Castle (EH – tel: 01833 38212) at Barnard Castle; Egglestone Abbey (EH) nearby.

Pubs and Cafés:
Pubs at Barningham and Kexwith.

The North Yorkshire Moors

Some riders believe that the North Yorkshire Moors offer the best offroad riding in England. Most of the offroad potential is concentrated in the western half of the National Park area, though further east you could try your luck on the trails of the Langdale Forest.

The most outstanding difference when comparing the North York Moors with the Yorkshire Dales and Lakes is that it may be tough getting up, but once you are up you tend to stay up for a long time. Furthermore the tracks that cross the moorland are often of the highest quality for riding, and this is partly due to the fact that the area is highly organized for shooting and all that goes with it. Grouse butts are a common sight – they do not get used very often, but if you get asked to stay away you should remember that these are the people who help to maintain the moors for everyone's enjoyment, and look for a ride elsewhere with a good grace.

Ride 19: Sutton Bank and the Hambledon Hills

Ride 20: Kepwick and the Boltby Circuit

Ride 21: Osmotherley and the Kepwick Circuit

Ride 22: From Chop Gate to Farndale

Ride 23: The Carr Ridge and Greenhow Moor

Ride 24: Roseberry Topping and the Captain Cook Monument

Ride 25: Spaunton Moor and Rosedale

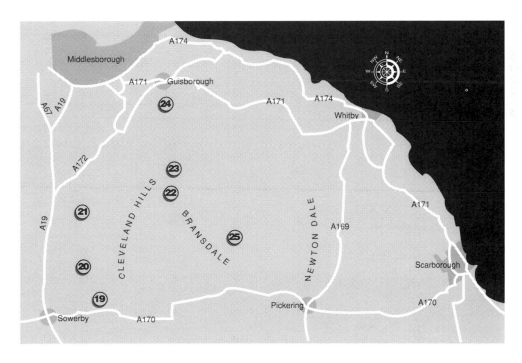

19 Sutton Bank and the Hambledon Hills

Offroad and On-Road

Area: The south-western corner of the North York Moors. Start and finish from the car park at the top of Sutton Bank by the side of the A170 between Thirsk and Helmsley.

OS Map: Outdoor Leisure 26 – North York Moors Western area; Landranger 100 – Malton, Pickering & surrounding area.

Route:
Sutton Bank CP (GR:518830)
Cold Kirby Road (GR:530844)
Old Byland (GR:552860)
Clavery Ley Lane/Lambert Hag Wood (GR:566856)
Barnclose Farm (GR:567872)
Ox Pasture Lane/Deep Gill Wood (GR:544878)
Peak Scar Road/Peak Scar (GR:530883)
Sneck Yate Bank (GR:508875)
Whitestone Cliff (GR:506838)
Dialstone Farm (GR:518843)
Sutton Bank CP (GR:518830)

Nearest BR Station: Thirsk.

Nearest Youth Hostel: Helmsley to the east along the A170.

Approx length: 15 miles (24km).

Time: Allow 2–3 hours, plus time for a visit to Rievaulx.

Rating: Moderate/Easy. The riding is mainly easy, and ends with a fantastic ride towards Sutton Bank. Finding the bridleway westwards from Barnclose Farm requires a little care and attention.

This circuit is a brilliant introduction to riding on the North York Moors; it is easily accessible and has the major advantage of starting high and staying high for most of the distance. It ends with a truly memorable ride along the edge of the heights from Sneck Yate Bank southwards towards Sutton Bank.

1. The Sutton Bank car park is easily found by the roadside at the top of Sutton Bank. From here follow the narrow road that goes northwards towards the radio mast, bearing right towards the hamlet of Cold Kirby which gives a fine, fast-wheeling downhill.

2. At the dead-end road sign for Cold Kirby you have an option; either turn left to head north along the Cold Kirby Road, or ride on ahead and try your luck on the short bridleway that follows the same direction. Then turn right onto Back Lane, and follow this quiet country road eastward into Old Byland.

3. Follow the road past the village green in Old Byland, turning right to continue west along Clavery Ley Lane which leads steadily down towards Lambert Hag Wood on the banks of the River Rye. Look out for a partly hidden turn to the left here, with signposts for both Tylas and Barnclose Farm.

3a. The big attraction is these parts is Rievaulx with its ancient Abbey, Temples and Terrace which is not more than 2 miles (3km) distant. If you want to divert there stay on the road and carry on down the hill to Rievaulx Bridge where you turn left uphill to Rievaulx.

4. The lane that leads to Tylas and Barnclose Farm is bridleway, though it is tarmac all the way as it follows the hillside to the north with a steady loss in height which makes it quite a fast ride in this peaceful, wooded valley. Watch out for the speed bumps, turning right downhill and then left past Tylas Farm; from here a short uphill takes you to Barnclose Farm,

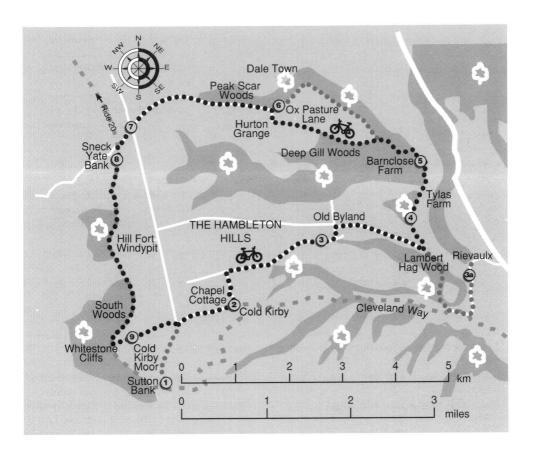

which offers bed and breakfast in a very pleasant setting.

5. The bridleway sign points left through a gate to a grass track going up the hill. This is where you can go wrong, and some care is needed with navigation. A short way up the hill the main track goes on ahead with two forks off to the right. The right turn is the way to go, following the side of a hedge up to the top of the hill to follow the bridleway along the side of Priest Wood and Hag Wood. From there you want the bridleway that heads west, either crossing a clearing to follow the north side of Deep Gill Wood through to Ox Pasture Lane, or alternatively following the south side of East

Ley and Cliff Wood.

6. Both bridleways come to the road close to Murton Grange. From here follow the Peak Scar Road westwards from Peak Top where you have the option of diverting offroad to Dale Town, and from there following the bridleway from Noddle End. The problem is that it is a long way down into the valley, with a long climb to get back out of it!

7. The Peak Scar Road continues westwards to Sneck Yate where at the first crossroads a right turn up a byway track will take you a mile or so to High Paradise Farm where you can connect with Ride 20. To continue with this

Moorland riding – there are times when it's easier to use a ladder than open and close the gate.

ride, head straight on from Sneck Yate, dropping a short way downhill to Sneck Yate Bank where a bridleway turns left marked as the Cleveland Way.

8. This bridleway gives a wonderful 3-mile (5km) ride along the top of the heights with fantastic views over the countryside to the west. It is easily followed and on the whole easy to ride all the way, as it passes the aptly named High Barn and Hill Fort Windypit en route for Whitestone Cliff. This is where the bridleway ends.

The track passes a bridleway heading down the side of the hill, and then you come to a headland that looks out over Gormire Lake and would make a fine place to stop and meditate. A short way on a sign says 'No Horses, No Bikes'. It is sad but sensible, as this part of Sutton Bank is best left to walkers and the hundreds of car-borne trippers who amble the short distance from the nearby car park.

9. Instead turn left up the side of the field, passing the solitary bridle gate which appears to have no role apart from showing the way. At the woods bear left round the side of the field, following the signposted direction to Dialstone farm along a good, fast track. Here you hit the road, bearing right for the start finish car park about 1 mile (1.5km) distant at the top of Sutton Bank.

Places to Visit:
Rievaulx Terrace and Temples
(NT – tel: 01439 798340);
Rievaulx Abbey
(EH – tel: 01439 798228);
Brymor Ice Cream (tel: 01677 460377)
at High Jervaulx Farm, Masham.

Pubs and Cafés:
Café at Sutton Bank car park.
No pub en route.

20 Kepwick and Boltby Circuit

Offroad and On-Road

Area: The western edge of the North York Moors. Start and finish from the car park at Kepwick, 2 miles (3km) to the east of the A19 to the north of Thirsk. Alternatively start and finish at Sneck Yate.

OS Map: Outdoor Leisure 26 – North York Moors Western area; Landranger 100 – Malton, Pickering & surrounding area.

Route:
Kepwick CP (GR:467908)
Cowesby (GR:466898)
Kirby Knowle (GR:468873)
Boltby (GR:489867)
Sneck Yate Bank (GR:508875)
High Paradise Farm (GR:503887)
Cleveland Way/Kepwick Quarry (GR:489914)
Thorodale Wood (GR:511904)
Dale Town Common (GR:512890)
Hambleton Road (GR:504890)
High Paradise Farm (GR:503887)
Gallow Hill (GR:484899)
Kepwick CP (GR:467908)

Nearest BR Station: Thirsk or Northallerton.

Nearest BR Station: Helmsley to the south-east on the A170; Osmotherley to the north off the A19.

Approx Length: 17^{1}/$_{2}$ miles (28km).

Time: Allow around 3 hours.

Rating: Moderate/Easy. The riding is easy, with the exception of the final bridleway that leads down into Kepwick. The length of the ride can be reduced by leaving out the Dale Town Common loop.

This route follows quiet roads, forestry tracks and the Cleveland Way to form a fine circuit on the western side of the North York Moors. It can be linked to Rides 19 and 21 to make a long-distance circuit which can be adapted to suit individual requirements.

1. Kepwick is an isolated and very attractive hamlet which can be reached by car from the A19 north of Thirsk. You are asked not to park on the grass verges, and should use the small car park next to the church. From here turn right along the road and turn westwards. You can either follow the road round to Cowesby to the south of Kepwick, or take the bridleway which goes steeply over the hill; the road is by far the easier option.

2. Keep south along Ruddings Lane to Kirby Knowle where there is a church and a manor house and not much else, and then follow the road through to Boltby. Again there is an optional bridleway which cuts off the corner, but the roads are so quiet and pleasant to ride on in these parts that it seems scarcely worth the hassle.

3. From Boltby follow the road to the north-east, and prepare for the long uphill struggle to the top of Sneck Yate Bank. About two-thirds of the way up a track is signposted to High Paradise by the side of Spring Wood; you can go this way, but I preferred to gain more height on the road which gets steep from here on, taking the left turning track near the top of Sneck Yate Bank which is signposted as the Cleveland Way and is the link point with Ride 19.

3a. A good optional start point for the ride is at the Sneck Yate crossroads a short way up the hill here. There is limited space to park by the start of the Hambleton Road byway that heads north towards High Paradise.

4. From Sneck Yate Bank the bridleway follows a track through woodland which offers

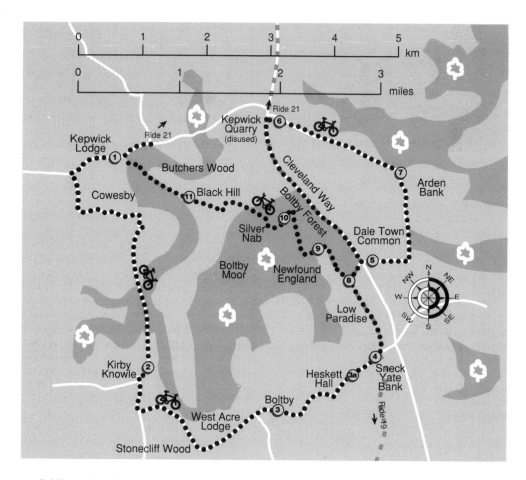

good riding; when it breaks out into the open it joins the main track that leads above Low Paradise to High Paradise. If you want to cut short the length of the ride, you can head straight through the forestry for Gallow Hill from here.

5. To continue with the main route that links on to Ride 21, head on up past the farm buildings at High Paradise, and then turn left onto the Hambleton Road/Cleveland Way. This excellent track follows the side of the forestry, then breaks out into open moorland at Steeple Cross. From here ride on past the trig point at 374m until you reach the clearly signposted

Kepwick Quarry/Cleveland Way crossroads by a gate in the wall.

6. This is where the route links to Ride 21, and you can see the Cleveland Way stretching ahead across the moorland to the north. However, turn instead onto the right-hand track which is signposted to the north-east, and follow it on an excellent fast surface across mainly level ground to the side of Thorodale Wood, passing through a few gates on the way.

7. Thorodale Lake can be glimpsed in the valley below; to its south, a bridleway turns off to the right across a grassy field leaving the wall by

Route-finding is mainly easy on the North York Moors, though an OS map and compass may be needed.

Some excellent tracks characterize this route, which gives mainly fast riding conditions.

the side of the woods, where a track carries on to the east. At first it is not that obvious to follow, but if you ride south across the field you come to a gate, and from there the track reasserts itself, passing through more gates before coming to a bridleway crossroads where it could easily be linked to Ride 00.

8. Turn right along the wall here, following the grass track due west to re-cross the Hambleton Road bound for High Paradise; the route enters Boltby Forest at the point where three official mountain bike routes also start, just below the farm: the 4-mile (6.5km) Green Route, the 7-mile (11km) Red Route and the 12-mile (19km) Blue Route.

9. The red route is the one to follow to reach the exit point at Gallow Hill, though if you enjoy woodland riding there is no reason not to take in the whole Blue Route which loops further south. The forestry tracks here are comparatively narrow and quite interesting, and as always with forestry it is quite easy to get lost because the trees blanket the view and destroy your sense of direction. So, just follow the Blue Route carefully, and after some steady ups and downs you should emerge on the north side of the forest at Gallow Hill, which gives a splendid view over the surrounding country despite its macabre connotations.

10. The most obvious track from here follows the side of the forest and turns south along Windygill Ridge. This is not the way to go, and

in fact the correct bridleway is not that easy to find in the summer as it is lost in the ferns at an unmarked crossroads with the bridleway that heads north away from the forest to join the Cleveland Way. If you come to a gate in a wall marked with a blue bridleway arrow you have come too far; go back a short distance and look for the hidden track that heads westwards.

11. This track soon heads down Black Hill below Gallow Hill, following a narrow, stone-littered track before breaking out into more open ground. However, it is very much single track all the way down, passing a footpath that goes into woodland before crossing Pen Hill, from where the track bears steeply right down the hillside of Atlay Bank to plunge down an extremely narrow track with rhododendrons on either side. This section is really not ridable, particularly if there are walkers about who must be given right of way, but it is only a short distance before an easier track levels off down the hillside, coming to a gate and from there heading to the road at Kepwick where you started the ride.

Places to Visit:
Nothing along the route;
Thirsk Museum and Rievaulx are within a few miles.

Pubs and Cafés:
No pubs or cafés along the route.

21 Osmotherley and Kepwick Circuit

Offroad and On-Road

Area: The western edge of the North York Moors. Start and finish from the car park at Kepwick, 2 miles (3km) to the east of the A19 to the north of Thirsk. Alternatively start and finish at Osmotherley, or at the Cod Beck Reservoir car park on a minor road to the north-east.

OS Map: Outdoor Leisure 26 – North York Moors Western area; Landrangers 100/99 – Malton, Pickering/Northallerton, Ripon & surrounding area.

Route:
Kepwick CP (GR:467908)
Cleveland Way/Kepwick Quarry (GR:489914)
Hambleton Street/White Gill Heads (GR:491932)
Solomon's Temple/High Lane (GR:476973)
Cod Beck Reservoir CP (GR:469993)
Osmotherley (GR:456972)
Thimbleby/Sandpit Lane (GR:448952)
Thimbleby Bank Plantation (GR:454947)
Over Silton (GR:452933)
Kirk Ings Lane/Bridge Beck Lane (GR:459924)
Kepwick CP (GR:467908)

Nearest BR Station: Northallerton.

Nearest Youth Hostel: Osmotherley.

Approx Length: 14¹/₂ miles (23km).

Time: Allow 2–3 hours.

Rating: Moderate. The ride starts with a steep on-road climb to join the Cleveland Way, and the route through Thimbleby Bank Plantation can be both muddy and confusing. Otherwise there should be no difficulties.

Another fine ride on the western fringes of the North York Moors; it divides almost equally between quiet roads and bridleway tracks, and links in with Rides 19 and 20 to the south.

1. From Kepwick follow the road eastwards as far as the imposing entrance gates of Kepwick Hall. Take the narrow lane that goes straight ahead by the side of the big wall here, and follow it east past the ford and the sign that says 'Not suitable for motors'. From here it is a steep uphill, breaking out onto the side of open moorland by a North York Moors plaque beside a gate. Keep on uphill by the side of Kepwick Quarry, eventually coming to a second gate set in a wall which signals the end of the tarmac.

2. This is the Cleveland Way/Kepwick Quarry crossroads which you also come to in Ride 20. Go through the gate and turn left, following the Hambleton Street/Cleveland Way track northwards across the moorland. It is easily followed across high ground with fine views over the lowlands to the west, but would be very exposed in foul weather.

3. After just over a mile (1.5km) the track bears north-west at White Gill Head above Whitestone Scar, dropping steadily downhill on a good surface to run along the side of the forestry plantation close by the Hambleton End trig point at 399m. Follow the track on to the north across Thimbleby Moor where it joins a bend in the road.

4. The road continues northwards across the moorland. About a mile further on take the track that goes straight ahead as the road bends left at Solomon's Temple. This is High Lane which takes you on a good surface past more forestry, before dropping downhill on a stone staircase – you need good technique to ride down here – to cross the beck a short way to the north-east of the Cod Beck Reservoir.

5. Join the road here. If you want another bridleway section you can continue north on the road from here, turning left (west) across Scarth Wood Moor on a bridleway and then following a bridleway south along the ridge of Swinestye Hill before joining the road by Ruebury Lane just to the north of Osmotherley. If you want the easy option with minimal climbing you can just follow the Quarry Lane road to the south-west past Cod Beck Reservoir, passing the track down to the Osmotherley Youth Hostel before riding down into Osmotherley.

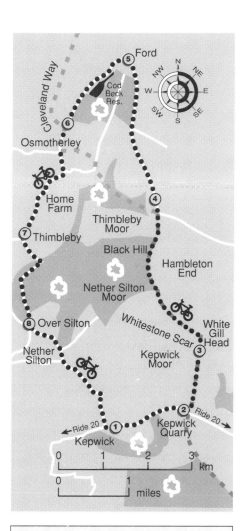

6. Osmotherley is a picture-postcard place and well worth a look round. Its attractions include three pubs, a fish and chip shop and at least two antique shops. From here follow the road south as it winds downhill to Thimbleby, and there on a clear right bend in the road look out for the bridleway that follows Sandpit Lane to the south-east.

7. This is clearly marked, and at first takes you on a fairly good track up to the forestry of the Thimbleby Bank Plantation. From here you need to take some care not to get lost and dis-orientated in the woods, and be prepared for plenty of mud and slippery branches if it has been at all wet. Follow the forest track to the right, and then bear left on a track that goes uphill to the Hanging Stone. From here it bears south towards Over Silton, though I found it none too easy to find the way out of the woods. You do not want the main track, which appears to bear round to the north-east: you want the narrow, single-track way that goes due south. It joins another track on the edge of the woods that will lead you down to the hamlet of Over Silton.

8. On the outskirts of Over Silton a bridleway heads across the fields via Greystone Farm to Silton Hall; this can be used to extend the offroad part of the ride, but in wet weather I preferred to stick to the road, which offers very pleasant riding. Follow Kirk Ing lane and Bridge Beck Lane to the south-east, and from there a final climb leads back up to Kepwick.

Places to Visit:
Remains of Mount Grace Priory (EH – tel: 01609 883494) to the north-west of Osmotherley, accessible by footpath from Osmotherley or by car/bike from the A19.

Pubs and Cafés:
Choice of three pubs and fish and chip shop in Osmotherley.

22 From Chop Gate to Farndale

Mainly Offroad

Area: The west of the North York Moors. Start and finish from the Chop Gate car park on the B1257 between Helmsley and Stokesley.

OS Maps: Outdoor Leisure 26 – North York Moors Western area; Landranger 100/93/94 – Malton, Pickering/Middlesborough & Darlington/Whitby & surrounding area.

Route:
Chop Gate CP (GR:558993)
Seave Green (GR:563002)
East Bank Plantation (GR:575004)
Tripsdale (GR:583989)
Stump Cross (GR:606982)
Cockayne (GR:620983)
Cow Sike (GR:625982)
Dickon Howe (GR:646974)
Monket House (GR:660972)
Farndale (GR:670975)
Hollins Farm/Daleside Road (GR:661984)
Elm House/Daleside Road (GR:642003)
River Dove/Farndale (GR:630009)
Bloworth Crossing/Cleveland Way (GR:616015)
Round Hill/Cleveland Way (GR:593015)
Medd Crag (GR:573010)
Bilsdale Hall (GR:566005)
Chop Gate CP (GR:558993)

Nearest BR Station: Northallerton.

Nearest Youth Hostel: Helmsley to the south along the B1257; Osmotherley to the west off the A19.

Approx Length: 20 miles (32km).

Time: Allow around 5 hours depending on your fitness, enthusiasm, technique and the riding conditions.

Rating: Moderate/Hard. This is a good distance over wild terrain, and it should only be undertaken in fine weather. There are four climbs in all, and in two of these there are sections where most bikers will have to get off and push.

If you want a single North York Moors 'Classic', this is probably the one. It takes you across wild country with a pub at either end, conveniently links with Ride 23, and is highly recommended for a fine day. It also opens the way for many more rides, as you discover the wealth of tracks and trails that lace the area.

1. Chop Gate has a convenient free car park (with amenities) to the south of the village. From here ride north along the B1257 past the llama and the pub; when the road starts to drop downhill take the first right turn at Seave Green signposted to the church at Town Green.

2. Turn immediately onto the bridleway, crossing the ford and following the track steadily up through fields past East Bank Farm. When the track bends right towards the buildings at East Bank House on the southern fringe of the woods you keep on uphill, following a narrow, fern-laden track through the edge of the woodland to enter the East Bank Plantation on the hillside.

3. Like much forestry, East Bank Plantation is not particularly easy to find your way through. Ignore the first inviting crossing track and keep on uphill, winding up through the trees to the second crossing track. Here you turn right for a short while, and then fork left onto another

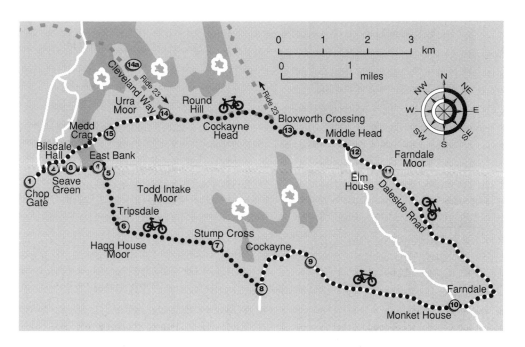

minor track that continues uphill – if you start to go downhill, it means you have overshot the turn-off.

4. Keep on uphill – you are probably pushing by now – until you break into the open on the eastern fringe of the trees. From here you have to go through a gate which can be appallingly muddy, bearing right to struggle up the steep but short hill ahead on a virtually non-existent track. This is positively the worst bit of the ride; rest assured that from here it will improve considerably.

5. Cross the ancient earthwork fortification that extends all the way along the top, and join a beautiful track that runs from north to south. Turn right to go south here, and follow it through the heather with fine views over to the west, ignoring the first track that turns off to the left. After a time the track follows the side of a wall on the right. When it starts to curve away from this wall, you turn 90 degrees left onto the clear track that heads east by a large stone edi-fice, and ignore the track that continues straight ahead across Nab End Moor.

6. This track soon starts to drop down into Tripsdale, zig-zagging down the hillside on a pleasing track that gets you to the bottom of the dale where an even steeper track leads up the other side. Once back on the top of Hagg House Moor you pass a couple of shooting huts which could make a good place to shelter in poor weather.

7. Continue across Slape Wath Moor to Stump Cross where you cross a major track running north to south by a pile of stones. Past here the track starts to head on a steady downhill and gives a fast ride, bringing you down to the road to the west of Colt House Farm where a bridleway sign shows that you have been riding in the right direction.

8. Turn left on the road, and follow it steeply downhill past Breck House and over the cattle grids to Cockayne at the head of the dale. This

The North York Moors are popular with riders who regularly use the old roads for a day out.

An isolated shooting hut can be a useful place to shelter if the weather closes in on top of you.

is a lovely place in an unforgettable setting, with just a church and a few houses. Follow the road round to the other side of the dale and start climbing, ignoring the bridleway sign to the left and looking out for the left-turning track just beyond opposite the farm buildings at Cow Sike.

9. This track leads up and over the hilltop to Farndale, a fairly easy climb is fairly easy on a good surface; it then levels out and crosses the Westside Road, another major track that runs north to south across the moorland. Beyond Dickon Howe it starts to drop downhill and the state of the track deteriorates until at Monket House Crags it resembles a ravaged lunar landscape with a few poles and posts by the side showing the way it used to be. Towards the bottom erosion has carved a spectacularly deep gulley; this can be avoided by following the side of the field on the way down to the road by the farmstead at Monket House.

10. Turn right on the road at Monket House, and then after a short distance turn left to cross the Thorn Wath Bridge to Farndale, where you will find the pub ready and waiting just past the halfway stage of this ride.

From here follow the dead-end Daleside Road uphill to the left, heading north-west along the hillside past Hall Farm, Hollins Farm and other isolated farmsteads in fine moorland surroundings.

11. At Elm House the tarmac road comes to an end. Follow the bridleway track round the back of the farm building, and on by the side of a wall towards the head of the dale. It then comes to a gate above the River Dove where careful navigation is required to get you up to the top at Bloworth Crossing on the other side. Turn left downhill and cross the bridge. Then immediately turn right up a narrow track towards an isolated barn, and at the top follow the track round to the left and downhill to cross another bridge.

12. This takes you up the other side, and it is not easy going. Follow the bridleway arrow, and keep on in the same direction until you come to a gate. You will almost certainly have pushed much of this section, and it could be very wet. At the gate a track heads on through the heather, but frequently disappears and then reasserts itself before some elderly grouse butts covered in heather show you are headed in the right way. Keep going west as the moor flattens out, and before long you will reach the Westside Road track which crosses the moor.

13. Turn right on the Westside Road, and then fork left at the Bloworth Crossing where you will find a Cleveland Way signpost and a lonely seat. This is also where the route links to Ride 23. Follow the Cleveland Way signpost at the next turning, taking the left fork down a bumpy track which then heads up to Cockayne Head and the high point of the ride at Round Hill on

Looking back down the hill to Cockayne, an isolated settlement that looks idyllic on a fine day.

a fairly good surface.

14. Look out for the Round Hill trig point (454m) which is about a hundred yards off to the right in the heather. The Cleveland Way follows the right fork here along the Carr Ridge here, while the left fork heads straight back to Chop Gate via Medd Crag.

14a. If you prefer to follow the Carr Ridge, it is possible to ride on to the gate at the top of the ridge, then double back by following the narrow bridle track that runs all the way along the earthwork fortifications heading south on the edge of Urra Moor towards Medd Crag. For those looking for a further challenge it makes an interesting ride which adds just over 2 miles (3km) to the total distance.

15. When the main track from Round Hill turns hard left, keep straight on down to Medd Crag, crossing the earthwork to join a rough, narrow track that heads on through a bridle gate and down the hillside past Weighill's Plantation and on to Bilsdale Hall. Here you reach the road, from where a fast downhill takes you to the B1257 at Seave Green, with the Chop Green car park no more than five minutes along this road.

Places to Visit:
Nothing in the immediate area; Helmsley Castle (EH – tel: 01439 770442) is nearby.

Pubs and Cafés:
Pubs at Chop Green and Farndale.

---

23 Carr Ridge and Greenhow Moor

Offroad and On-Road

Area: The west of the North York Moors, to the south-east of Great Ayton off the A173. Start and finish from the Carr Ridge forestry car park just off the B1257.

OS Map: Outdoor Leisure 26 – North York Moors Western area; Landrangers 93/94 – Middlesborough & Darlington/Whitby & surrounding area.

Route:
Carr Ridge CP (GR:572034)
Carr Ridge/Cleveland Way (GR:583025)
Round Hill (GR:594016)
Bloworth Crossing/Cleveland Way (GR:616015)
Burton Howe/Greenhow Bank (GR:607032)
Tidy Brown Hill (GR:602050)
Battersby Moor (GR:607066)
The Park/Cleveland Way (GR:606086)
Kildale (GR:607093)
Battersby (GR:596077)
Ingleby Greenhow (GR:582064)
Carr Ridge CP (GR:572034)

Nearest BR Station: Kildale or Battersby Junction; Northallerton.

Nearest Youth Hostel: Helmsley to the south along the B1257; Osmotherley to the west off the A19.

Approx Length: 16 miles (26km).

Time: Allow 2–3 hours.

Rating: Moderate. The initial climb to the Carr Ridge is a horror story, but after that everything gets better. The ride neatly divides into two halves, the first offroad, the second on-road.

This is a fine ride across the moors of the Cleveland Hills, but the catch is that you have to get to the top before you really get started. After that it has the makings of a perfect offroad blast for mile after mile, eventually dropping to the road at Kildale where it links with Ride 24, and from where a lowland ramble takes you back to the start point.

1.   The car park just off the B1257 below Carr Ridge makes a good place to start this ride which is pure offroad for the first half of the route. Alternatively you could start from Kildale or Battersby Junction, which both have railway connections from the east. From the car park head south along the B1257 for a short distance, reaching the brow of the hill where you turn left through a gate onto a bridleway track as signposted for the Cleveland Way.

2.   The track is quite easy to begin with, but as it starts to climb steeply its surface becomes a carefully constructed stone staircase. This may be great for walkers, but for bikers becomes ridiculous as they struggle to push and carry their machine up the hill. Never mind. No more than half a mile into the ride the agony is over, and you go through a gate at the top of the staircase to follow the Carr Ridge on a good track that heads fairly gently up to the 454m trig point at Round Hill, where you could link into Ride 22.

3.   Follow the track due west on past Cockayne Head where a track bears off to the left. This is not the way to go as it joins the old railway that once crossed the moor, but it could be worth investigating as not far on it leads to Incline Top, where it plunges straight down the hill. It is fearsome from the top, and even more fearsome when you consider that some local tyros challenge each other to ride 'The Incline' non-stop to the top.

4.   Continue on the correct route to Bloworth Crossing where you again link with Ride 22, before turning left at the Cleveland way sign-

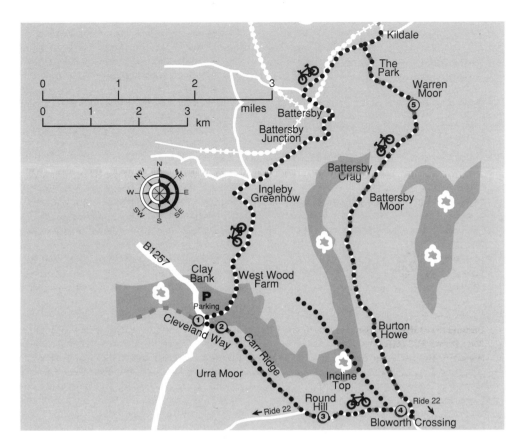

post to follow the splendid track that heads north across the moorland on the top of the hill. This offers great riding past Burton Howe and Greenhow Bank, though inexplicably is not labelled as bridleway between Bloworth Crossing and Tidy Brown Hill. Ignore side turnings and it is easy to follow, with fine views to the west and north, crossing Battersby Moor on a plunging downhill to meet a dead-end road and a small car park – slow down for walkers – above Baysdale Farm.

5. Go through the gate and join the road, which gives a memorable downhill past The Park and eventually leads to the road on the outskirts of Kildale. Here you can turn right and search out the tea house in this hamlet, or turn left and continue to ride which follows quiet lowland roads back to the start point via Battersby and Ingleby Greenhow. Riding along Lamb's Lane and Greenhow Avenue gives fines vies of The Incline in the distance, and then to finish there is a short but strenuous uphill back to the start point.

> **Places to Visit:**
> Nothing in the immediate area;
> Captain Cook Schoolroom and Museum in Great Ayton to the north-west.
>
> **Pubs and Cafés:**
> Tea house at Kildale; no pubs en route.

24 Roseberry Topping and the Captain Cook Monument

Area: The north-west corner of the North York Moors. Start and finish from the Pinchinthorpe Station Guisborough Forest car park on the A173 to the west of Guisborough, or from Great Ayton.

OS Map: Outdoor Leisure 26 – North York Moors Western area; Landranger 93/94 – Middlesborough & Darlington/Whitby & surrounding area.

Route:
Pinchinthorpe Station CP (GR:583153)
Hutton Lowcross Woods (GR:590137)
Roseberry Mines (GR:582123)
Airy Holme Farm (GR:578117)
Dikes Lane (GR:577109)
Captain Cook's Monument bridleway (GR:590096)
Mill Bank Wood (GR:600100)
Sandbeds Plantation (GR:604100)
Kildale (GR:607093)
Quarry Hill/New Row (GR:618102)
Percy Cross Rig (GR:613114)
Hutton Moor (GR:598129)
Hutton Gate (GR:596143)
Pinchinthorpe Station CP (GR:583153)

Nearest BR Station: Great Ayton.

Nearest Youth Hostel: Osmotherley to the south-west off the A19.

Approx Length: 12 miles (19km).

Time: Allow 2–3 hours.

Rating: Moderate/Hard. The distance is short, but there is some hard riding offroad which makes it a taxing circuit.

This route takes in two major local landmarks – the hill known as Roseberry Topping and the Captain Cook Monument at the top of Easby Moor. It offers some challenging riding with the option of extending the route in a variety of directions, as well as linking to Ride 23.

1. Guisborough Forest has a single official cycle route which starts from the old Pinchinthorpe Station where there is a large free car park. Nothing of the old station remains except the platform, and the railway has been transformed into a walkway which starts off the ride. Turn left along the old railway track, taking care to give way to walkers. At the second gate turn right up into the forest by a permissive path sign.

2. This brings you up to a wide forestry track. Turn left here, and follow it through the forest past a couple of houses, bearing right through a gate by open ground to head up into High Bousdale Wood. From here follow the track as it zig-zags north and south again, eventually leading out of Hutton Lowcross Woods by the side of Hanging Stone Wood by the north-west corner of the forest.

3. You cannot miss the great lump of Roseberry Topping ahead. Keep on towards it, and then follow the track which bears round its left (east) side across Roseberry Common, crossing the Cleveland Way at a gate. Ride straight ahead here, following the bridleway downhill past the old Roseberry Mines to Airy Holme Farm, which was once the home of the explorer Captain James Cook. Bear left round the front of the farmhouse to join a lane that continues on to the road at Dikes lane on the outskirts of Great Ayton. Captain Cook spent much of his youth here, and in the town you can visit his celebrated schoolroom and museum.

4. Cross straight over Dikes Lane towards Southbrook Farm to join a narrow bridleway that heads up the hillside before breaking out

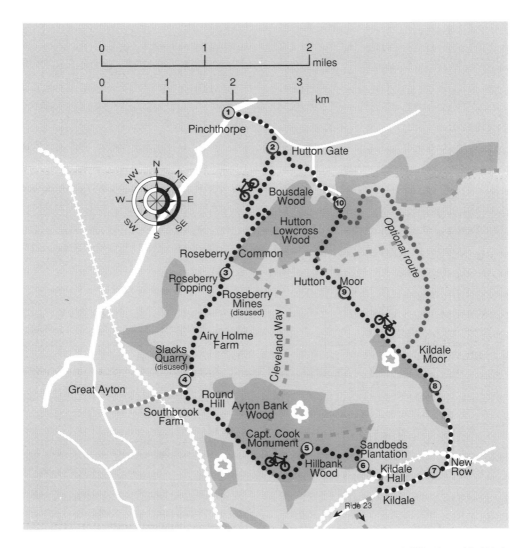

into the open below Round Hill. From here it follows the contour lines all the way round the hillside to Bankside Farm above Kildale, and is alternately pleasant and frustrating riding. The Captain Cook Monument is on the hillside above, but if you want to pay your respects it can only be approached by footpath.

5.   After a while the wide, grassy track deteriorates into a narrow track through high ferns which can be narrow and difficult to ride if it is wet and muddy under your wheels. Keep straight on and ignore all turn-offs, eventually heading into the main forest at Bleach Mill Intake where it is important to follow the main track even if you are not convinced it is going the right way. This gives an enjoyable up and down ride, soon bringing you out of the forest at Sandbeds Plantation where you turn right down the hill by Bankside Farm.

The edge of the forest with Roseberry Topping in the background. Most of the tracks are easy to find.

Roseberry Topping dominates the landscape for miles around and is well worth exploring on foot.

6. Follow the lane downhill from Bankside Farm, crossing the railway line and coming to the road at Kildale where in season you will find a tea house. This is where you can connect with Ride 23. Turn left along the road past Kildale Hall, and after about half a mile take the first left turn signposted to New Row.

7. Follow the narrow dead-end road back across the railway line towards the terrace of cottages at New Row, and then join the track that goes up through the woods on a steep and bumpy surface. At the top this brings you out to the road at Percy Cross Rig on Kildale Moor; turn left here, and follow the dead straight road in a north-westerly direction along the side of the Lonsdale Plantation.

8. If you want to extend the ride, you can turn right at the next bridleway, following a track which heads down across the moor to Sleddale Farm and up across the Codhill Heights to Hutton Village. Alternatively keep straight on along the road, passing a monument to the man who discovered some ancient tumuli which are unique in Yorkshire, and then joining a track which goes straight on at the end of the road.

9. Follow this track north-west to Hutton Moor, where it starts to drop downhill towards the Guisborough Forest. At first it is easy riding, but as it enters the forest the track gets lumpier and bumpier, mainly due to the piles of old bricks and other building materials that have been dumped onto the track in a misguided attempt to prevent erosion. The track, which is bridleway, heads north all the way towards Hutton Village, but if you do not like technical descending you will be better off turning west to rejoin the official cycle route.

10. The bridleway eventually reaches the road on the outskirts of Hutton Village. Turn left here towards Hutton Gate, and after the right-hand bend take the track on the left signposted as bridleway to Home Farm. This leads across low ground back to the fringes of the forest, reconnecting with the outward route with no more than a few minutes' pedalling to get you back to Pinchinthorpe Station.

Places to Visit:
Captain Cook Schoolroom Museum
in Great Ayton
(tel: 01642 722208/723556).

Pubs and Cafés:
Tea house at Kildale;
no pubs en route.

25 Spaunton Moor and Rosedale

Offroad and On-Road

Area: The central southern area of the North York Moors. Start and finish from car park at Hutton-le-Hole, 2 miles (3km) to the north of the A170 near Kirkbymoorside.

OS Map: Outdoor Leisure 26 – North York Moors Western area; Landranger 94 – Whitby & surrounding area.

Route:
Hutton-le-Hole CP (GR:705903)
Spaunton Moor/road (GR:717930)
Royal Oak Inn (GR:724955)
Daleside Road/Thorgill (GR:707966)
Daleside Road/Moorlands Farm (GR:693989)
Daleside Road/Hill Cottages (GR:708976)
New Road/Rosedale Abbey (GR:726958)
Royal Oak Inn (GR:724955)
Hollins Farm (GR:733943)
Spaunton Moor/Lastingham Ridge bridleway (GR:725930)
Lastingham (GR:730904)
Hutton-le-Hole CP (GR:705903)

Nearest BR Station: Malton.

Nearest Youth Hostel: Helmsley approximately 9 miles to the west along the A170.

Approx Length: 17 miles (27km).

Time: Allow 2–3 hours plus stops.

Rating: Moderate/Easy. Navigation is very straightforward and if the tracks are dry the offroad sections will be easy, but be prepared for a push to the top of Spaunton Moor.

This is a highly enjoyable figure-of-eight circuit taking in both Spaunton Moor and Rosedale, and the riding is easy enough to offer a relaxed introduction to the area suitable for those with modest aspirations. Note that Hutton-le-Hole is a popular village, likely to get very busy with car-borne visitors in the high season – so start early.

1. If you are starting from Hutton-le-Hole, the car park on the northern outskirts of the village is very convenient. Alternatively you could start the ride from Rosedale Abbey which has a small car park, or make your own route from Helmsley where the youth hostel is warmly recommended as a good base for the area.

2. From the Hutton-le-Hole car park turn right uphill on the road, and then take the first left fork to follow the road which crosses Spaunton Moor from south to north. This gives an up-and-down ride through a barren landscape though you are gaining height all the way until you reach the viewpoint above Rosedale. When I rode across here in less than good weather no cars were encountered; however, if the road is busy with cars you may prefer to follow the Lastingham Ridge offroad return route across the moor.

3. The Rosedale panorama is also the start of a dramatically steep on-road descent into the valley. With some parts of the hill as steep as 30 per cent cyclists are told to 'dismount' and are then presumably expected to walk down, but if you have faith in your brakes and take it easy on the bends you should have no problems riding down to the Royal Oak Inn which signals the next turn-off.

4. Do not overshoot the left turn on the downhill opposite the pub here. It is signposted to the Golf Club, following the Daleside Road on a narrow lane that gives an easy ride along the hillside as it passes a few houses along the way.

5. This lane finally weaves its way to Thorgill,

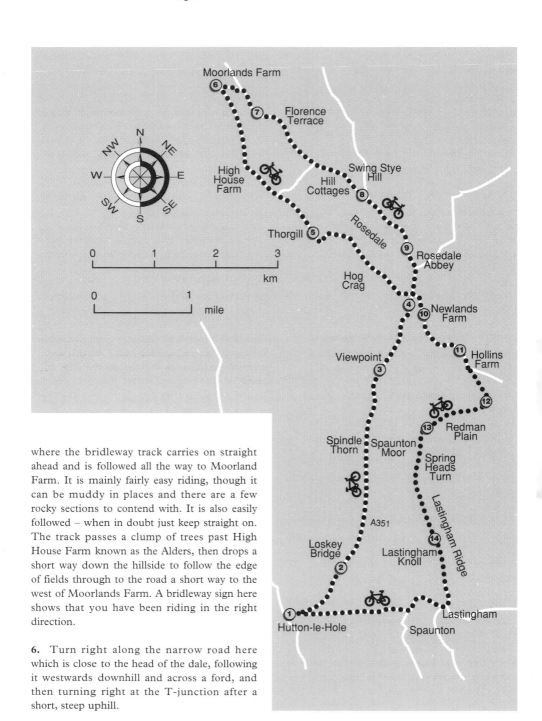

where the bridleway track carries on straight ahead and is followed all the way to Moorland Farm. It is mainly fairly easy riding, though it can be muddy in places and there are a few rocky sections to contend with. It is also easily followed – when in doubt just keep straight on. The track passes a clump of trees past High House Farm known as the Alders, then drops a short way down the hillside to follow the edge of fields through to the road a short way to the west of Moorlands Farm. A bridleway sign here shows that you have been riding in the right direction.

6. Turn right along the narrow road here which is close to the head of the dale, following it westwards downhill and across a ford, and then turning right at the T-junction after a short, steep uphill.

7. From there follow the Daleside Road to the south-west as it swoops along the hillside, with some good down hills soon bringing you to Hill Cottages opposite a phone box. Here a bridle-way heads north up the hillside, which could provide an interesting variation on the route if you are so inclined.

8. The next stage takes you on to Rosedale Abbey, which is reached in record time after some excellent on-road downhills – one pleas ing feature of this ride is that there does appear to be more down than up. Rosedale Abbey can be a busy little place and has a pub, tea house and village shop, as well as a car park which makes it a possible alternative start point for the ride.

9. The turn-off from Rosedale Abbey to head south back to the Royal Oak Inn is easily missed; it is best to turn right past the green, and then follow the road round to the left to the entrance of the caravan park where you turn right up a narrow lane. Ride steeply uphill to the pub, and then take a left through its car park opposite the golf course turn-off of the outward route, following the track ahead.

10. This track is easily followed along the hill-side past Newlands Farm and a couple of smart houses at Bank Farm. Further on it goes close by an isolated pottery shop, before it heads up to the ruined buildings of Hollins Farm where the gate ahead is tied up and a blue bridleway sign tells you to turn right along the wall.

11. After the dramatic downhill into Rosedale you might expect a grim haul back to the top again. Surprisingly it is not at all bad, though most riders will find it too steep to pedal in all but the easiest sections. The track clearly bears up by the Hollins Farm wall, passing between two marker stones. Where you have a choice of following the wall or turning right up the hill-side, the latter route is the one that leads across Spaunton Moor to Lastingham.

12. The views over Rosedale are very fine from here. After a relatively short distance a narrower track turns uphill to the right; this is the way to go, leading you steeply up to Redman Cross, with the bridleway following a narrow path cut through the heather, which is easy to ride once you have managed the hill. A few grouse butts are passed as the path joins a wider moorland track heading in a westerly direction which eventually brings you to a crossroads marked by a large cairn.

13. It is important to get the direction right at this crossroads: carry on straight ahead, which should have you following a wide track which swings south towards Spring Heads Turn. It is downhill nearly all the way, with the track smooth enough to offer fairly fast riding though watch out for the drainage channels that are cut across it. An exhilarating ride will bring you along the Lastingham Ridge to Lastingham Knoll, with the track getting wider, rougher and potentially muddier as it closes on the edge of the moor.

14. When you reach a gate ride down the road into the hamlet of Lastingham, turning right and right again past the Blacksmith's Arms pub to follow the road westwards with its gentle ups and downs as it brings you back to the start point of Hutton-le-Hole.

Places to Visit:
Ryedale Folk Museum at
Hutton-le-Hole (tel: 01751 417367).

Pubs and Cafés:
Pubs at Hutton-le-Hole,
Rosedale Abbey and Lastingham;
cafés at Hutton-le-Hole
and Rosedale Abbey.

Cycling Books from the Crowood Press

Great Cycle Routes – North and South Downs   Jeremy Evans

Great Cycle Routes – Dartmoor and Exmoor   Jeremy Evans

Great Cycle Routes – Dorset and the New Forest   Jeremy Evans

Great Cycle Routes – Wales and the Borders   Jeremy Evans

50 Mountain Bike Rides   Jeremy Evans

Adventure Mountain Biking   Carlton Reid

Cycle Sport   Peter Konopka

Offroad Adventure Cycling   Jeremy Evans

Touring Bikes   Tony Oliver

Mountain Biking – The Skills of the Game   Paul Skilbeck

Cycling on Road and Trail   Jeremy Evans

The CTC Book of Cycle Touring   Les Woodland

Cycling in France   Tim Hughes